"I strongly recommend this book to all who are interested in improving their relationships with others."

—JOHN WOODEN
former head basketball coach, UCLA

"An exciting, power-packed book. I want all my staff to read and discuss it together."

—LLOYD OGILVIE, pastor
Hollywood Presbyterian Church

"A winner! McGinnis knows how to help people discover all that life holds for them."

—BRUCE LARSON, author
There's a Lot More to Health than Not Being Sick

"Unless you live in isolation, this is a must-read book!"

—DENIS WAITLEY, author
Seeds of Greatness and *The Double Win*

"To the extent that leaders are made, not born, this book will help to make them, as well as anything I know."

—DAVID HUBBARD, president
Fuller Theological Seminary

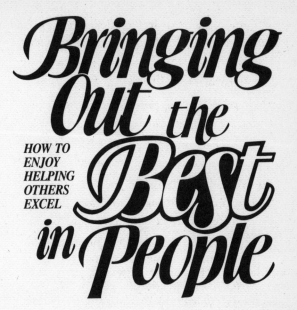

Bringing Out the Best in People

HOW TO ENJOY HELPING OTHERS EXCEL

ALAN LOY McGINNIS

AUGSBURG Publishing House • Minneapolis

BRINGING OUT THE BEST IN PEOPLE
How to Enjoy Helping Others Excel

Copyright © 1985 Augsburg Publishing House

Library of Congress Cataloging in Publication Data

McGinnis, Alan Loy.
  BRINGING OUT THE BEST IN PEOPLE.

  Bibliography: p.
  Includes index.
  1. Motivation (Psychology)   2. Psychology, Applied.
I. Title.
BF503.M44   1985   153.8   84-28400
ISBN 0-8066-2150-8
ISBN 0-8066-2151-6 (pbk.)

Manufactured in the U.S.A.   APH 10-0922

                                                     5   6   7   8

Dedication

This is a book about teaching people to succeed and it is dedicated to a man who does not need to read it, Mr. William B. Carruth.

When Carruth arrived at the Friendswood School one sweltering day in September 1949, he must have been a little bewildered at the ragtag group of kids he found there. It took only one building to house all 12 grades, the library comprised less than 200 volumes, and there were so few students that a new teacher was given a wide array of subjects: history, geography, civics, English.

Mr. Carruth was one of a whole stream of men who returned from the war in a hurry to make up for lost time. He knew exactly what he wanted to be—a teacher. That meant returning to college, and it meant he would be 33 before facing his first class. He had no illusions, I hope, that he would ever make much money working in the small towns of Texas. But when he appeared before us that day, we could tell that he was eager to begin and that he meant business. Yet there was a glint of mischief in his eyes too, which made him hard to size up. Perhaps that was part of his appeal—there was always a certain mystery to his past and his personality that kept us off guard. Perhaps it was the energy and enthusiasm he brought to his teaching. Or perhaps it was the way he leaned back in his chair after school, his hands clasped behind his head, listening to a little knot of farm children talk on and on about their dreams and fears. At any rate, I was nuts about him after the first month, and would have followed him anywhere. That was 35 years ago, but I still recall many of those conversations— where we stood, what he said, how I felt.

Mr. Carruth has long since left teaching and now lives in quiet retirement in Houston, where I hope that he finds some refreshment in the recollection that he invested the best years of his life in some children.

Also by
Dr. Alan Loy McGinnis

Books

Confidence (Minneapolis: Augsburg, 1987)
The Romance Factor (San Francisco: Harper & Row, 1982)
The Friendship Factor (Minneapolis: Augsburg, 1979)

Audiocassettes

Confidence: How to Succeed at Being Yourself (Glendale, CA: Valley Counseling Center, 1987. An album of 12 audio talks by Dr. McGinnis based on the book *Confidence* on envisioning a confident self.)

Motivation without Manipulation: Bringing Out the Best in People (Glendale, CA: Valley Counseling Center, 1985. An album of 12 audio talks by Dr. McGinnis based on the book *Bringing Out the Best in People* containing additional new information not in print.)

The Romance Factor (Glendale, CA: Valley Counseling Center, 1985. An album of 12 audio talks by Dr. McGinnis based on the book *The Romance Factor,* a handbook on love and marriage.)

How to Get Closer to the People You Care For (Glendale, CA: Valley Counseling Center, 1981. An album of 12 audio talks by Dr. McGinnis based on the book *The Friendship Factor* containing additional new information.)

Alan Loy McGinnis may be contacted at Valley Counseling Center, 517 E. Wilson Ave., Suite 204, Glendale, CA 91206, (818) 240-9322.

Contents

12 Rules for
Bringing Out the Best
in People

1 Expect the best from people you lead.

2 Make a thorough study of the other person's needs.

3 Establish high standards for excellence.

4 Create an environment where failure is not fatal.

5 If they are going anywhere near where you want to go, climb on other people's bandwagons.

6 Employ models to encourage success.

7 Recognize and applaud achievement.

8 Employ a mixture of positive and negative reinforcement.

9 Appeal sparingly to the competitive urge.

10 Place a premium on collaboration.

11 Build into the group an allowance for storms.

12 Take steps to keep your own motivation high.

Acknowledgments

Thanks to the following persons who have read pages from this book and have made very helpful suggestions: Dale and Marlene Benecke, David Bower, Bill Carruth, Rev. Edward Danks, Dr. Dennis Denning, Thomas Edwards, Pat and Jane Henry, Don and Cherry Henricks, Robert Hughes, Dr. Taz Kinney, Tricia Kinney, Richard Laskin, David Leek (in many many versions, always with great care), Alan McGinnis Jr., Kent and Sherie Newell, Dr. Walter Ray, George Rybak, Theodore Saenger, Mike Scroggie, Nancy Smith, Mary Alice Spangler, Dr. Robert Swinney, Sandra Swinney, and Wendell Will.

Particular thanks to Mike Somdal, who, in addition to being a valued friend, has a good ear for the language and knows rot when he hears it. The following persons have been good to help with research: Mary Ellen Draper, Nury Godoy, Rena Inman, Sherry Kirtley, and Lisa Wood.

Most of all I'm grateful to Diane. Being a writer is fun, but I've never known anyone who claimed it was fun to be married to one. Somehow Diane wears that mantle with grace and equanimity.

Cases from my practice are sufficiently scrambled and coalesced so that patients will not recognize themselves. The topography of their lives, however, is accurate.

Preface

After the publication of my first book, *The Friendship Factor,* I began to get some strange requests. Corporation heads would call, saying, "We're having trouble motivating our employees—especially the younger ones—and we need you to come and speak to our executives." At first it seemed presumptuous for a family therapist who knew almost nothing about business to try to tell such leaders how to run their companies. But since most of my research and writing had been about how people can get along with each other better, I began to look for ways to help business people apply these principles.

The cognitive psychologists were making some good discoveries about motivation, but I was certain that the most sound suggestions on how to inspire people would be found in history. So I ransacked biographies as far back as Alexander the Great to learn how effective leaders have inspired others to go the second mile. My research revealed that there are only about a dozen principles of motivation and that successful people were using them long before psychology had a name. Moreover, I discovered that for all the millions of words written about him, Jesus had rarely been studied from this perspective—a curious fact when you realize that he was clearly the most successful motivator of all time.

So the seminar, "How to Bring Out the Best in People," was born, and it turned out to be rather popular. At first I gave these lectures to top-level executives in such companies as IBM, and the longer I worked with management the more I saw that in our high-tech world the crying need seems to be for managers with people skills, who know how to eliminate friction in their offices and inspire excellence among their staffs.

And then the topic proved to have even wider application. We found that most of us use the same techniques of motivation at home that we use at the office, and mothers, it turned out, were more interested than anyone. I discovered that virtually everyone is a motivator in one situation or another—when we're persuading a friend to lose weight, or giving a pep talk to our kids, or trying to help a batter out of a slump, we're motivators. Either we are doing it poorly or we are doing it well.

It is the purpose of this book to pass on to you principles which will enable you to do it well. If you will incorporate them into your everyday dealings with people, I am convinced that you will find yourself getting ahead at a surprising rate. What is more important, the people around you will be very grateful. For our chief want, as Emerson said, is someone who will inspire us to be what we know we *could* be.

*"The most powerful weapon on earth
is the human soul on fire."*
—FERDINAND FOCH

CHAPTER ONE

The Psychology of Motivation

Have you ever wondered at the way certain people bring out the best in others? They seem to know how to get an extra effort from the people they lead. We have all known them— some are teachers or heads of companies, others are baseball managers or mothers. Frequently without good looks or extraordinary intelligence, they seem to possess a knack for inspiring people. And this remarkable skill at the art of motivation makes them highly successful at almost everything they do.

On the other hand, there are those who seem to bring out the worst in us. When we are around certain people we feel clumsy and inept and find ourselves acting in negative ways that puzzle us later. Their pep talks end up becoming lectures, and though they may intend to inspire us, they actually intimidate us.

The Sources of Inspiration

My work as a psychotherapist has furnished me with opportunities to observe these various pulls we have on each other and to ponder the sources of inspiration. When I met people who were peak performers, I often asked, "What motivated you? Who first got you on the right track, and how did they do it?" In gathering this information and in reading the biographies of great leaders, I began to see that in business, in politics, in a family—indeed in any venture—motivation breaks down to a few very powerful principles. It turns out that a coach like Bear Bryant, a businessman like Lee Iacocca, and a religious leader like Mother Teresa use many of the same tools for energizing their people and that their groups respond in very similar, predictable ways. In the succeeding chapters we will look at the stories of dozens of successful leaders and the methods they have used to obtain an extraordinary effort from ordinary human beings. I hope to show how you can employ these methods in day-to-day relationships.

The 12 guidelines contained in this book are quite simple. They can be mastered by anyone with enough desire to inspire others. I'm not saying that they are *easy* skills to learn, for changing our relational habits can be very difficult, and mastering the art of motivation takes a lot of hard work. But with enough persistence, anyone can become an expert in this field. Motivators are not born—they are made. And they are almost always self-made.

The Power of the Motivator

We must deal immediately with a wrongheaded idea now circulating widely about this topic. It says that no one motivates anyone and that all motivation must come from within. But think about the times when you have been at your best. Was it not due in large part to the influence of some inspiring person? Perhaps it was a teacher who knew how to pull something extra from you and got you so excited about a project that you stayed up most of the night reading, or a boss who could make work fun and had a knack for putting together a team in which people found themselves producing beyond their usual capacities. Wellington reportedly said that when Napoleon was on the field, it was, in balance, the equivalent of fighting against another 40,000 men. The fact is that we can be *highly* motivated by the right leader.

When France fell to Hitler in June of 1940, it seemed that for the second time in 25 years the lights were going out all over Europe. Germany immediately began preparations for an invasion of the British Isles, and the prospects for successful resistance looked very bleak. The Soviet Union stood aside, the United States was far from being ready to enter any war, and most military experts predicted that England, poorly armed and poorly prepared, would topple to an invasion within weeks. But the experts made those predictions without taking the measure of a 65-year-old politician who, after an erratic and frustrating career filled with failures, had finally been handed the post of prime minister on May 10. The seven remaining months of 1940 were a pivot of modern history. England—and perhaps the whole Western world—owes its existence to the ability of Winston Churchill to breathe hope into a dispirited and frightened nation during those months.

To appreciate the power of the motivator one need only picture the families of Britain as they gathered in their living rooms and listened to Churchill thunder out from their radios:

The Battle of France is over. I expect that the Battle of Britain is about to begin. Upon this battle depends the survival of Christian civilization. The whole fury and might of the enemy must very soon be turned on us. Hitler knows that he will have to break us on this island or lose the war. . . .

Let us therefore brace ourselves to our duties and so bear ourselves that, if the British Empire and its Commonwealth last for a thousand years, men will still say: "This was their finest hour."

Looking back on England's heroic defiance of Hitler, most would agree that indeed it *was* England's finest hour. But that heroism could have lain dormant in the British people had not Churchill been so successful at galvanizing their will.

The Longing for Inspiration

History shows that in almost every arena there is a vacuum waiting to be filled by some person who can impart vision and steer people's energies into the best endeavors.

Some leaders assume that people are basically lazy and do not want to be inspired. That assumption can be heard in sales managers' voices when they say that nothing seems to build a fire under their salespeople, or in a teacher's lament, "Harry is just not motivated!"

"But there is no such thing as an unmotivated person," says R. J. Wlodkowski, a professor of education at the University of Wisconsin. "It is more accurate to say, 'Harry is not motivated to learn with me.' " For Harry will spring out of bed at three o'clock on the morning of a fishing trip and display plenty of motivation. Watching factory workers hurry out of a parking lot at the end of the shift quickly dispels any notion that they are inherently lazy. They are in a rush to get to evening activities, some of which will probably be more taxing than anything they have done at the factory.

So the leader's challenge is not to take lazy people and transform them into industrious types. Rather it is to channel already existing energies into the most worthwhile endeavors. People do not like being lethargic and bored. They will welcome the manager who can teach them to enjoy their work, or the teacher who will impart to them a love of learning that causes the school day to go swiftly.

How One Mother Inspired Her Children

The Lazy B Ranch is comprised of 260 square miles of scrub brush on the New Mexico and Arizona border and has been in the Day family since 1881. When Harry and Ada Mae Day were ready to have their first child, they traveled 200 miles to El Paso for the delivery, and Ada Mae brought her baby, Sandra, home to a difficult life. The four-room adobe house had no running water and no electricity. There was no school within driving distance. One would have thought that with such limited resources, Sandra's intellectual future was slim.

But Harry and Ada Mae were dreamers who did not allow themselves to be limited by their surroundings. Harry had been forced by his father's death to take over the ranch rather than enter Stanford University, but he never gave up hope that his daughter would someday study there. And Ada Mae continued to subscribe to metropolitan newspapers and to magazines such as *Vogue* and *The New Yorker*. When Sandra was four, her mother started her on the Calvert method of home instruction and later saw that she went to the best boarding schools possible. Sandra's brother Alan says that one summer their parents packed them in the car and they drove to all the state capitols west of the Mississippi. "We climbed to the dome of every building until finally we had to come home," he said.

Sandra did go to Stanford, then on to law school, and eventually on to become the first woman Supreme Court justice in the United States. On the day of her swearing in, the Day family was there, of course. During the ceremony Alan watched her closely as she put on her robe, then walked to her seat among the justices. "She looked around, saw the family and locked her eyes right into ours," said Alan. "That's when the tears started falling."

What causes a woman like Sandra Day O'Connor to go so far? Intelligence, of course. And lots of inner drive. But much of the credit goes to a determined little ranch woman sitting in her adobe house at night, reading to her children hour after hour, and to parents scampering up the stairways of capitol domes, their children in tow.

Motivation Is Not Manipulation

Before going any further we must make it clear that the topic before us is not manipulation. In the last decade a spate of books has been telling us how to get ahead by intimidating people and stepping on the bodies of our subordinates. You have wasted your money on this book and would be well advised to return it to the bookseller if you are looking for techniques for twisting people into doing your bidding. This is a book on *motivation*, not manipulation. The difference is this. You are a manipulator when you try to persuade people to do something that is not in their best interests but is in yours. You are a motivator when you find goals that will be good for both sides, then weld together a high-achieving, high-morale partnership to achieve them.

Why Every Business Person Must Be a Psychologist

One's financial success is much less dependent on hard work and knowledge than it is on the ability to lead people. Many bright persons rise rapidly in their careers because of their high-tech knowledge. But once they arrive at a level where they have to succeed through the efforts of others, they get mired down simply because they have not learned the art of multiplying themselves. One industrial psychologist says that promotions are 90% dependent on technical know-how for a rank-and-file worker. For promotions as supervisor, technical knowledge is 50% and human relations are 50%. For promotions as executive, technical expertise is 20% and human relations are 80%. An almost total switch in skills takes place as people rise higher on the management ladder.

The German poet Goethe observed, "The greatest genius will not be worth much if he pretends to draw exclusively from his own resources." Yet this law is ignored by a surprising number of hard-working people whose careers have not been kissed by success. They've failed to accomplish big things because they have failed to master the art of inspiring others. Those who get ahead sometimes have limited gifts themselves, but their people consistently turn in superior performances. And that is because, though these leaders do not necessarily work long hours, when they do work they use their time organizing and motivating people.

"Great [corporate] leaders understand human behavior rather than the cybernetics of any functional specialty," says James Schorr, executive vice-president of Holiday Inns Inc. Translated, what he is saying is that a proven motivator will make it to the top before a proven genius. When Andrew Carnegie hired Charles Schwab to administer his far-flung steel empire, Schwab became the first man in history to earn a million dollars a year while in someone else's employ. Schwab was once asked what equipped him to earn $3000 a day. Was it his knowledge of steel manufacturing? "Nonsense," snorted Schwab. "I have lots of men working for me who know more about steel than I do." Schwab was paid such a handsome amount largely because of his ability to inspire other people. "I consider my ability to arouse enthusiasm among the men the greatest asset I possess," he said, and any leader who can do that can go almost anywhere and name almost any price.

Building High Morale

Thus far we have been discussing the art of motivation as a one-to-one skill—the impact of one personality on another. But for most of the people with whom we work, there is another set of influences operating, and unless the motivator learns how to control these influences, no amount of one-on-one leadership will be effective. I am referring to the power of the peer group.

A curious chemistry takes place when you put three or more people together to make a family, a class, or a corporation: those people begin to exert complicated powers over each other. Some groups, for instance, seem prone to producing destructive electricity. A few disgruntled employees or a group of critics in a club— left unattended—can create a strong negative field in a hurry. Unless the leader is skilled in defusing those influences, the whole organization can explode.

How does one keep such negative feelings from gaining momentum? There are two ways. The first is a secret employed by all morale builders: they build into the group an allowance for conflict. They do not panic when negative emotion occurs—they expect it, and they are prepared for it. Morale problems rarely get out of hand for these leaders because they have constructed corridors of communication for the disgruntled student or the unhappy employee to use. In the chapters that follow we will discuss at some length the art of managing conflict and how to get groups to cooperate with a minimum of sparks.

When Critical Mass Occurs in a Group

There is a second secret used by skilled motivators. They carefully put together combinations of people that will ensure a positive mental set from the beginning. The principle is this: enthusiasm is contagious, and people are motivated when we place them in contact with other well-motivated people. Eventually, when the optimism reaches a high enough temperature, the fire becomes self-generating. So the wise leader, upon discovering people who are peak performers, will quickly put them in touch with each other. Like a burning charcoal, an enthusiastic person can ignite others and create a fine fire. Left alone, the flame will eventually go out.

Let's take the example of company presidents or the heads of large volunteer organizations. If they depend on their enthusiasm alone to fire up their people, they will be moving about their organizations in a constant frenzy. But wise leaders use the dynamics of crowd psychology much more in meetings. They know that they can get 10 people more inspired at a meeting with the right tone than in 10 one-to-one conversations. So they construct a *group* of positive thinkers in regular contact with each other who will then keep each other's faith alive. At some point, critical mass occurs. A strange and wonderful thing can happen when such groups reach this critical mass: they generate an enthusiasm which is much greater than the sum of the parts.

The power of this group spirit has been emphasized by several recent studies of companies such as 3M, Frito-Lay, Procter and Gamble, and IBM. The research shows that these companies have been able to succeed in good times and bad because they build a distinctive "culture" within their organizations. The new employee in such companies learns that "there is a way we do things here." This atmosphere of strongly shared objectives and values points people in the right direction, eliminates confusion, and saves time.

Such *esprit de corps* exists in all successful families as well. Certain family units seem to generate a morale that sends kids out to function at levels far above average. Outsiders may make the mistake of crediting these children's success to inherited I.Q. when actually it is due to far more than intelligence. It comes from the energy and enthusiasm that are generated from within the family group. As at the best corporations, a common culture is formed in these families. They join in striving for common goals and they promote greatness in one another.

The Complexity of Inspiration

No one knows all the reasons why one group jells into a successful team and another turns into a suicidal mob. Nor do we know all the reasons some individuals have a desire to excel and others lack it. There are variables of energy and physiology, of psychological history, and of time and place. This book does not pretend that by using one magical technique you can turn a slow-learning child into a genius, or a nonperforming employee into a barnburner. What these principles *will* help you do is to inspire people to make a greater effort than they would ever have attempted without you.

For 12 years the Green Bay Packers had won only 30% of their games, and by 1958 their record had dropped to a dismal one and ten. Then in 1959 along came a new coach—Vince Lombardi. During Lombardi's nine-year reign the Packers had nine winning seasons, beat their opponents 75% of the time, and walked away with five NFL championships, including the first two Super Bowls.

How does one account for such a phenomenal turnaround? Frank Gifford says it was not Lombardi's knowledge, since several other coaches knew as much about strategy and tactics. Rather, it was his ability to motivate the players. "He could get that extra ten percent out of an individual," Gifford says. "Multiply ten percent times forty men on the team times fourteen games in a season—and you're going to win."

In this book we are going to look at the success stories of many leaders who, like Lombardi, knew how to obtain an extra effort from the people around them. By using their principles you should be able to get an extra 10% from your group. And that just may be the difference that wins the game.

> *"The chief lesson I have learned in a long life is that the only way to make a man trustworthy is to trust him; and the surest way to make him untrustworthy is to distrust him and show your mistrust."*
> —HENRY L. STIMSON

> *"Attitudes are more important than facts."*
> —KARL MENNINGER, M.D.

CHAPTER TWO

Expecting the Best

Three months after retiring from a direct-sales company where she had worked 25 years, Mary Kay Ash decided to start her own company. Her attorney and many friends thought she was crazy to invest her life savings of $5000 in a foolhardy idea for a cosmetics firm, but Mrs. Ash had some strongly held beliefs that she thought would work in the corporate world.

After only 20 years the company recorded $323.8 million in sales in 1983, and over the previous five years had averaged more than a 40% return on equity. That is among the highest in American industry. One figure for her company is absolutely unique: there are more women earning over $50,000 per year at Mary Kay Cosmetics than at any other company in the world.

What is the secret of such success? In part it lies in

the remarkably positive attitude Mrs. Ash displays toward every person on her staff. "I wanted to create a company that would give women an opportunity to accomplish anything they were smart enough to do," she says, and she apparently thinks that the people who work for her are smart enough to do anything. When one enters the gold, glass building which houses the home offices of the firm, larger-than-life photographs of the national sales directors stand out. "While some companies use paintings or sculptures or perhaps images of their products to make a statement," Mary Kay says, "we want our message to be: 'We're a people company.' "

Unfortunately, when many people become leaders they take a different tack and quickly find themselves frozen into the role of police officers. Because of superior knowledge and experience, they think it is their duty to look over people's shoulders, to watch for errors and discourage cheating. They are there to prevent failure. By adopting such a watchdog role, they quickly set up an adversarial relationship, and people will follow such bosses with all the relish of going in for a root canal. Good managers and good teachers, on the other hand, do not waste much time doing postmortems on the failures of their people. Instead they look for strengths that others have overlooked and ways to encourage the gifts in their group.

More than anything else, it is our attitude toward the people in our classroom or office that will determine failure or success at motivation. If people know we expect good things from them, they will in most cases go to great lengths to live up to our expectations. If we expect the worst, they will meet those predictions with disappointing accuracy.

So rule number one for becoming a good motivator is this:

*E*XPECT THE BEST FROM PEOPLE YOU LEAD

In Toronto some time ago, I gave a speech to an executive club, and after the meeting an elderly man came up to talk. He was tall, slender, and elegantly dressed. At 74, he was retiring from a lifetime of manufacturing lead pencils. I thought to myself, "What a boring way to make a living," and said, "I'll bet you're glad to be getting out of that business, aren't you?"

"Oh no," he replied. "In fact, I'm going to miss it like crazy. And you know what I'm going to miss most? The friends I've made in this business. Some of my suppliers and customers have been my best friends for 40 years. And several of our upper-level managers are guys I hired right out of college. I've had a lot of satisfaction helping them succeed."

As we talked, I learned that this man had built up a multimillion-dollar company and had recently sold it for a very large sum. His success should not be all that surprising, however, considering his deep-rooted belief in people. He had mastered the art of finding the good side of everyone and building on that. And in the process of helping other people succeed, he had made a lot of money as well.

In any business that involves others—either as your employees or as your customers—attitude is everything. In the simplest terms, the people who like people and who believe that those they lead have the best of intentions will get the best from them. On the other hand, the police-type leader, who is constantly on the watch for everyone's worst side, will find that people get defensive and self-protective and that the doors to their inner possibilities quickly close.

How to Turn Your Child into a Thief

More and more psychological studies show that we have the power to call out the worst or the best in people by our expectations. The executive who believes "you just can't get good help anymore" and the teacher who is convinced that most kids are lazy hold a remarkable negative power over those people.

Psychologist C. Knight Aldrich, who worked for years with delinquent children, wrote a fascinating article some time ago in a psychology journal explaining how parents can quickly turn their children into thieves. Here's the way to do it. Let us say that your son—as most children do at some time or another—engages in some petty theft. Perhaps he steals a package of candy. If you say to him, "Now we know what you are—you're a thief! We'll be watching you from now on," it is quite likely that he will steal more and can quickly graduate from stealing candy to stealing cars.

On the other hand, you can react with both firmness and gentleness by saying, "Tom, that wasn't like you at all. We'll have to go back to the store and clear this up, but we're not going to make a huge thing of it. What you did was wrong, you know it was wrong, and we're sure you won't do it again." After such treatment most kids' stealing careers are over. The principle is very old: by assuming a negative attitude and reflecting back to people all the data about their weaknesses, you put them in touch with their faults and their behavior becomes worse. By assuming a positive attitude and concentrating on their strong aspects, you put them in contact with their good attributes and their behavior becomes better.

Believing the Best Intentions

A 17-year-old patient sat in my office some time ago and said sourly, "I'm so tired of being told that I don't live up to my potential. Every time a teacher starts in on that routine, I want to throw up. My dad says it about once a month."

This young man is a typical product of high-achieving parents (his father is a physician) who have a terrible time with both their employees and their children because they expect the same sort of drive in everyone else. They are trying to inspire their son, but the result is defiance. Here is why. Saying "You have great potential" is a compliment to his talent, but they have quickly jerked it away with the remark, "You don't live up to your potential." In the process they have attacked his character, which is much more serious. Each of us, no matter how derelict, wants to believe that we have the best of intentions, and we want others to believe that as well.

The Pygmalion Effect

In George Bernard Shaw's play *Pygmalion* the professor helps a slattern by the name of Eliza Doolittle become an elegant lady. He does this primarily by treating her like a lady at all times until she begins to live up to his expectations of her. Goethe stated the principle this way: "Treat a man as he appears to be, and you make him worse. But treat a man as if he already were what he potentially could be, and you make him what he should be."

A famous study in the classroom by Robert Rosenthal, a Harvard psychologist, and Lenore Jacobson, a San Francisco school principal, furnishes us with a good illustration of this. They asked the question: Do some children perform poorly in school because their teachers expect them to? If so, they surmised, raising the teacher's expectations should raise the children's performances as well. So a group of kindergarten through fifth-grade pupils was given a learning ability test and the next fall the new teachers were casually given the names of five or six children in the new class who were designated as "spurters"; the tests supposedly revealed that they had exceptional learning ability.

What the teachers did not know was that the test results had been rigged and that the names of these "spurters" had been chosen entirely at random. At the end of the school year, all the children were retested, with some astonishing results. The pupils whom the teachers thought had the most potential had actually scored far ahead, and had gained as many as 15 to 27 I.Q. points. The teachers described these children as happier, more curious, more affectionate than average, and having a better chance of success in later life. *The only change for the year was the change in attitudes of the teachers*. Because they had been led to expect more of certain students, those children came to expect more of themselves. "The explanation probably lies in the subtle interaction between teacher and pupils,'' speculates Rosenthal. "Tone of voice, facial expressions, touch and posture may be the means by which— often unwittingly—teachers communicate their expectations to their pupils. Such communication may help a child by changing his perceptions of himself.''

Centering on Strengths Rather than Weaknesses

Most of the people who come under our influence will have within themselves a mix of good and bad, ambition and lassitude, strengths and weaknesses. We can choose whether to build on their strengths or become obsessed with their weaknesses. I talked once to a layman in a very successful church. The pastor who had led that congregation for more than 20 years had some glaring faults, but the people seemed to love him and the parish had prospered. I asked the man how he accounted for this, and here is the very wise thing he said: "Our minister has some strong suits and he has some weaknesses. So we have tried to specialize in the areas where he is strong and forget about his weaknesses.''

By taking such an attitude the congregation had done two things: (1) they had avoided the backbiting and carping atmosphere which often exists in a church or a business where there is continual criticism, and (2) with such a generous spirit, they had doubtless motivated their pastor to do everything in his power to produce at full capacity. The result? A remarkable partnership which has produced results year in and year out.

The Pleasure of Discovering Hidden Talent

When we elect such a positive view, lots of buried talent begins to surface. Elbert Hubbard said, "There is something that is much more scarce, something finer far, something rarer than ability. It is the ability to recognize ability." Average people have a way of accomplishing extraordinary things for teachers and leaders who are patient enough to wait until ability becomes apparent.

The history books are full of stories of gifted persons whose talents were overlooked by a procession of people until someone believed in them. Einstein was four years old before he could speak and seven before he could read. Isaac Newton did poorly in grade school. A newspaper editor fired Walt Disney because he had "no good ideas." Leo Tolstoy flunked out of college, and Werner von Braun failed ninth-grade algebra. Haydn gave up ever making a musician of Beethoven, who seemed a slow and plodding young man with no apparent talent—except a belief in music.

There is a lesson in such stories: different people develop at different rates, and the best motivators are always on the lookout for hidden capacities.

One chief executive officer, when asked, "What are you in business for?" replied, "I am in the business of growing people—people who are stronger, more autonomous, more self-reliant, more competent. We make and sell at a profit things that people want to buy so we can pay for all this." It is not by accident that his employees, who probably would grumble about working eight hours a day for mere food and shelter, cheerfully work 10 and 12 hours a day for a leader who keeps such goals clearly before them.

A Climate in which to Grow

We can render the people around us a great service if we can provide an environment in which they not only can discover their gifts but also develop them. Theodore Roosevelt wrote, "There are two kinds of success. One is the very rare kind that comes to the man who has the power to do what no one else has the power to do. That is genius. But the average man who wins what we call success is not a genius. He is a man who has merely the ordinary qualities that he shares with his fellows, but who has developed those ordinary qualities to a more than ordinary degree."

People need an atmosphere in which they can specialize, hone their skills, and discover their distinctiveness. The biographies of the great are sprinkled with accounts of how some teacher or some kindly employer looked closely enough to see a spark no one else saw and for periods, at least, believed in their ability to perfect that gift when no one else did. The Taft family, for instance, was evidently good at pushing their children to cut their own swath and to find a specialty of which to be proud. When Martha Taft was in elementary school in Cincinnati she was asked to introduce herself. She said, "My name is Martha Bowers Taft. My great-grandfather was President of the United States. My grandfather was United States senator. My daddy is ambassador to Ireland. And I am a Brownie."

The Nature of the Human Spirit

It is quite important to understand that the attitude with which we approach people will be largely fashioned by what we believe about the nature of the human race. Douglas McGregor, a pioneer in the field of industrial psychology, became more optimistic about human nature the more he studied it. Attacking what he called "Theory X"—the authoritarian view of management which assumes that people are morons who need to be told what to do—he advanced "Theory Y," the theory which treats people as individuals and respects their human rights. Abraham Maslow's research corroborated McGregor's theories of management. A psychologist at Brandeis University, Maslow was particularly interested in peak experiences—what he called the "higher ceilings of human nature." The more research he did on these phenomena, the more convinced he was that people have much greater potential than we give them credit for. "There's more of the transcendent, the altruistic, the idealistic in many more people than I had ever suspected," he wrote.

In graduate school I was exposed to some very bleak theories on the nature of mankind and read philosophers who saw *homo sapiens* as quite depraved. But the longer I talk to people in my counseling chambers—especially when they are under hypnosis or tell me their dreams—the more I am convinced that human nature has often been sold short. I see the worst sides of thousands of people, yet I believe more than ever in the possibilities of the human spirit.

One reason I can be more tolerant than most is that as a therapist I have the advantage of information about my patients that most people are not privy to. And I discover that we rarely if ever see the totality of another in ordinary social intercourse. When an individual appears mean and lazy, we are only seeing one part of the person, elicited by a particular set of circumstances on a particular day, and we do well to wait a while before concluding that what we see is the whole person.

When People Change

Some pessimists would say that no one changes, that the leopard never changes his spots. But in fact everyone is changing every day, either for better or for worse. Here is a young CPA sitting in my office, asking about his mother, who is a patient at our clinic. As he talks about himself I learn that his career is soaring, that he has recently become a partner in one of the big eight accounting firms. "Most people would have a hard time believing that I spent almost four years whacked out on drugs," he says, "but it's true." He goes on to explain how that ended because of the woman he fell in love with almost nine years ago, and as he sits here in my office, healthy, alert, and successful, I realize what foolish cynicism it is to say that people never change. *Of course* they change, and we can influence, to some extent at least, how they change.

The Capacity for Stretching

We will be able to take a more positive view toward our group by remembering what an enormous capacity everyone has for stretching. William James said:

> Everyone knows on any given day that there are ener-
> gies slumbering in him which the incitements of that
> day do not call forth. . . . Compared with what we
> ought to be, we are only half awake. Our fires are
> damped, our drafts are checked. We are making use
> of only a small part of our possible mental and physical
> resources. . . . Stating the thing broadly, the human
> individual thus lives far within his limits; he possesses
> powers of various sorts he habitually fails to use.
>
> It is evident that our organism has stored-up reserves
> of energy that are ordinarily not called upon—deeper
> and deeper strata of explosible material, ready for use
> by anyone who probes so deep.

That remark was not made by some shouting motivational speaker at a marketing conference. It was
made by the dean of American psychologists. His concepts are important not only for what they say about
the untapped potential in us, but also for what they
say about uncovering the potential energy *in those
around us*. If James was anywhere near right, people
are capable of a remarkable amount of stretching, and
in our circle of acquaintances resides a pool of power
waiting to be released and harnessed.

When Dwight D. Eisenhower was president of Columbia University, he called John Erskine "the greatest teacher Columbia ever had." Erskine was one of
the most versatile men of his era—educator, concert
pianist, author of 60 books, head of the Julliard School
of Music, popular and witty lecturer. Writing about
that remarkable career, his wife Helen attributed it to
his "defiant optimism." He was a good teacher, she
said, because of "his own excitement for learning and

his trust in the future.'' He would tell her often, ''Let's tell our young people that the best books are yet to be written; the best paintings have not yet been painted; the best governments are yet to be formed; the best is yet to be done by *them*.''

Capitalizing on the Desire to Succeed

It may seem an obvious fact, but so many leaders ignore this simple truth that I must state it explicitly: no one wants to be a failure. Nearly all of us want to succeed. ''Every man believes that he has a greater possibility,'' Emerson said, and all my patients, no matter how depressed and down, seem to believe that they are capable of something better. They may be behaving terribly and performing poorly, but they want to do better, and there are reasons, they say to themselves, for their present poor performance.

To the scornful, such rationalizations are lame excuses, and it is easy to say that such persons will never live up to their talk. The road to hell is paved with good intentions, such sceptics are fond of saying. But the point is this: deep in the breast of everyone there is a drive to achieve something, to be somebody. And therein is a wonderful entry point for the motivator. If you will tap into that drive and demonstrate that you believe in people's futures, they will do almost anything to live up to your expectations. And they will work harder for you than for anyone else in the world. Bill Hewlett, one of the founders of Hewlett-Packard, said, ''Our policy flows from the belief that men and women want to do a good job, a creative job, and that if they are provided with the proper environment they will do so.''

"She Wanted Me to Succeed More Than I Did"

I was once waiting to speak at a sales conference when the year's awards were being given to the outstanding salespeople. One woman, who had performed spectacularly that year and who had made an extraordinary amount of money, gave all the credit to her sales manager. As she stood before a crowd of 3000 people, clutching the award for best producer of the year, she recalled the slump she had been in two years previously. The future had looked so bleak that she was ready to resign and had even called her supervisor several times to quit. But the manager kept persuading her that she had not tried long enough, that she would not have been hired if there had not been unusual potential in her. Her voice cracked as she related that story. Then she made this insightful remark: "For all those months when I wanted to quit and didn't think I had any future, Joan believed in me more than I believed in myself. She wanted me to succeed even more than I did."

That sales manager had effectively employed our first rule of motivation: Expect the best from people you lead.

*"We must give to every will to live the same reverence
for life that we give to our own."*
—ALBERT SCHWEITZER

CHAPTER THREE

*A Tailor-Made Plan
of Motivation*

*T*homas Aquinas, who knew a great deal about education and motivation, once said that when you want to convert a man to your view, you go over to where he is standing, take him by the hand and guide him. You don't stand across the room and shout at him; you don't call him a dummy; you don't order him to come over to where you are. You start where he is, and work from that position. That's the only way to get him to budge.

This principle can be seen at work in the remarkable success of life insurance salesman Frank Bettger. He was a professional baseball player with a glass arm who had to change careers, so he decided to try selling life insurance. It did not go well, and at 29 he was a miserable, debt-ridden failure. Then, improbable as it sounds, he became so successful in the field that he was in a position to retire at age 41. Bettger attributes this turnaround to a change in his selling approach, due in large part to a talk he heard at the Bellevue-Statford Hotel in Philadelphia. The speaker was one of America's top salesmen, J. Elliott Hall. Hall told how he also had failed as a salesman and was about to give up when he discovered the reason *why* he was failing. He said he had been making "too many positive statements."

"That sounded silly," says Bettger, "but it caused me to sit up and listen." Hall explained that his mistake had been to spend too much time trying to extol the product and too little time asking questions of the prospective customer. "Hall's questions had only one purpose," says Bettger, "*to help the other people recognize what they want, then help them decide how to get it.*" That idea revolutionized Bettger's attitude toward selling. "Before this," he said, "I had largely thought of selling as just a way of making a living for myself. I had dreaded to go in to see people, for fear I was making a nuisance of myself. But now, I was inspired! I resolved right then to dedicate the rest of my selling career to this principle: finding out what people want, and helping them get it."

So rule number two for bringing out the best in people is this:

MAKE A THOROUGH STUDY OF THE OTHER PERSON'S NEEDS

Too many leaders ignore this essential early step. They see motivation as mere hype—slapping people on the back and giving rah-rah pep talks. But it is much more than hype. A good motivational plan must be as carefully fitted as a designer dress, and before starting a program of leadership and change, it is important to study our clients carefully. We must ask a lot of questions about where people have been and where they are going, what they believe, what are their sore spots, what they love and what they hate. In other words, we must make an inquiry into people's present need systems. Freud did us a great favor in showing that all behavior is caused and everyone is motivated. So if people are already driven by a bundle of desires, we can avoid much frustration and failure if we study them very carefully to see how we can best appeal to their interests.

Frank Bettger tells how he applied this principle in his church. Elected superintendent of a small, struggling Sunday school, he thought the important immediate need was for a larger organization, so he asked for five minutes on the program during the following Sunday morning service. "I knew I had to make a sale," he explains, "and I *could* have got up and told the congregation that this job had been wished on me and I would expect them to cooperate and help me, but I decided that I would have a much better chance of getting what *I* wanted, if I talked to them about what *they* wanted."

Here is what Bettger said:

I want to talk to you for just a few minutes about some of the things you want. Many of you have children. You want them to come here to Sunday school and meet other children and to learn more about life from the truths in the great Book. You and I want our children to avoid some of the mistakes that I have made, and possibly some you have made. How can we do this?

The only way we can do it is by building a larger organization. You now have only nine teachers in the Sunday School, including the pastor himself. We need at least twenty-five. Some of you may hesitate to teach because you have the same fears that I had only twelve months ago when I took a small class of boys—that you don't know enough about the Bible. Well, I can tell you, you'll learn more about this Book in six months by teaching these little children for twenty minutes each Sunday morning than you will ever learn in six years by merely listening—and it will do more for *you*!

You husbands and wives can study and prepare the lessons together. It will give you something more in common, bring you closer together. If you have children of your own, they too will take a greater interest when they see you active. Remember Jesus' parable about the three men who were given the talents? I don't know of any better way you can improve and multiply your talents than through this work.

What happened as a result of Bettger's little speech? That morning they signed up 21 new teachers. At first there were not enough children to go around, so they divided them up. Some classes started off with only two or three. Then they began a house-to-house canvass, enrolled nearly every child in the community of Wynnefield, Pennsylvania, and eventually they built a large new church.

Different People Have Different Needs

I've been saying that the real winners succeed by learning the needs of other people, then appealing to those needs. Zig Ziglar, consultant to many marketing companies, puts it in even stronger terms: "You can get everything in life you want if you just help enough other people get what they want." But it is easy to make a fatal error at this point and assume that other people have needs identical to yours or that you can predict their needs without asking or listening. A professor of business tells about being poorly managed by his department chairman. One spring the chairman called him in and explained that they were not going to be able to raise his salary, but that they would give him tenure a year early, and reduce his teaching load.

"He said it as if it were some big deal," says the professor, "but what he didn't know was that I have a very low need for order. I like to live in a world of mild chaos—that's when I can do my best work. And I never like to know what's going to happen in the future. So tenure, which evidently meant a lot to this guy, was no carrot at all for me. If anything, it was a liability. And as to reducing my load, if he had been paying any attention at all to me, he would have noticed that I loved teaching so much that I would have paid for the privilege if I could. Had he talked to me about making some sacrifices in order to improve our department and challenged me to take on a *heavier* load, I probably would have jumped at the chance. If he had taken the trouble to find out a little more about me, he could have been a lot more successful in motivating me."

Beliefs

If we are to individualize our leadership, we will also want to find out what a person believes. In supervising younger therapists and talking over their patients' situations, I'm often surprised that they pay so little attention to belief systems. I suppose they have been taught in graduate school to stay away from theological discussions, and they make the mistake of thinking that the good therapist spends the whole session talking about "feelings" and never discusses beliefs.

As if the two were separable. So much of a person's emotional life and behavior stems from the convictions at the core of his or her existence. As M. Scott Peck says, there are people who say they have no religion and yet have very pronounced views of the world. For example, if a person sees the universe as basically a dog-eat-dog world where one must fight to survive, the therapist—or anyone who wants to motivate that person—must know that. If, on the other hand, people are pacifists, we may not want to use military imagery in trying to motivate them.

Many of my patients will say, when asked about their beliefs, that they are confused. "That's one reason I'm in therapy," they will retort with some exasperation, "I have no idea what I believe." For such persons I have a very simple assignment. Before our next session I ask them to write down at least 20 things about which they are certain. The items do not have to be world-shaking pronouncements—simply some things they know to be true or some things they love or hate.

One engineer said on his first visit to my office that he didn't know if there was anything wrong with him or not, but he'd been crying a great deal and sometimes slept through the weekend. He had grown up in an orthodox Christian home, then rebelled, and now called himself an agnostic. "Everything seems so relative," he said. "Morals have all changed, standards have all changed, and I feel as if I'm doubting everything and believing nothing."

Perhaps he thought I would preach at him about returning to his faith, but instead I asked him to go home and make a list of things he believed. "If you're not sure about certain religious beliefs," I said, "lay them aside for now, and concentrate on the things you're sure about." When he returned the following week, he was carrying in his hand a notebook, and his eyes had lost some of their hollow look. He was a little embarrassed, he said, because the list was "such a hodgepodge." The notebook contained such statements as these:

- Animals deserve to be treated kindly.
- I'm happiest when I live near the ocean.
- Sex is great.
- It's important to tell the truth.
- Careful craftsmanship is always good and sloppy work always causes trouble.
- I love my kids more than anything.
- Hate is always wrong and love is always right.
- Kindness to someone in trouble is awfully admirable.

He went on to say that he felt better to have discovered, after a little introspection, that he actually *did* believe in some things and that there were some convictions with which he could operate—even while plagued by doubt. As that engineer and I have worked together, his list has grown and a number of his old discarded beliefs have returned. He has even returned to church.

But my point is this: all people have belief systems, however buried, and until we get some idea of that configuration, until we learn what people value and what they want in life, we cannot expect to build a successful plan for motivating them.

Questions

Some very aggressive people appear to have only outgoing lines of communication; they barrage the people around them with data and pep talks and instructions. But the great teachers have incoming lines as well. They ask questions and they listen carefully. We all like to think of ourselves as good listeners, but the fact is that we speak at about 120 to 180 words a minute and think at four or five times that rate. So our attention wanders and we often pick up only about half of the other person's message.

At times it is very difficult for us to listen without judging. University of California psychiatrist Dr. Barbara Shipley says it is essential to show people that while you may not approve of their behavior, they are important as persons. Listening does this. "When a teenager walks in at 3:00 A.M., it's not easy for concerned parents to keep in mind the importance of listening. The impulse is to shout, 'I don't want to *hear* what happened!' But that attacks the other person's dignity, and if we determine to listen before judging, it will stand us in good stead later."

We Can Tell Where They're Going from Where They've Been

To understand what causes people to do what they do, it is also necessary to look at their past. We are, as Tennyson has Ulysses say, "a part of all that we have met," and we can tell a great deal about our people by where they have been and how their cultural history differs from our own. When a corporation head calls my office about a seminar and says, "We're having trouble motivating our employees," I can predict before going that they do not know their junior employees as well as they should. In nine cases out of ten, the managers are assuming that their younger staff come from a similar culture to theirs and that the same incentives which have always motivated the managers will do the same for their employees. But that is a dangerous assumption. Dr. Layne Longfellow says that most of the decision makers in business today are products of the Depression. Either they or their parents worried about basic needs such as food and shelter, and this powerfully shaped their value system. So when they were asked to work overtime, they always said, "Sure," thinking, "You never know when you'll need some more money, and we're lucky to have a good job."

But when one talks to baby-boomers about working overtime they say, "No thanks, but I *would* like to talk to you about another day off." They respond this way because their needs are simply different. To them work is important, but so is leisure, and the job takes second place to the quality of life. If one job doesn't work out, they know that there are plenty of others.

There is another thing about these workers' past that distinguishes them. Unlike many top-level managers, younger people were born into a world where people half expect a nuclear holocaust in their lifetime. They were very disillusioned by the assassinations of the Kennedys and King, and they were probably left confused by Vietnam and Watergate. So why should they sacrifice now to enjoy the rewards of old age when they may not have an old age? All our tugging and cajoling will be of little use until we take into account the forces that have shaped them.

Changing Needs

In addition to looking at people's pasts, it is also essential to recognize that everyone's need system is in a state of flux. This can be either a bane or a blessing, depending on one's viewpoint. For many employers it is a constant irritant—their people never seem to be satisfied. When labor leader Samuel Gompers was asked what the unions really wanted, he replied, "I can tell you what we want in one word: more." And some parents and managers suppose that their group has a similar attitude. "No matter how hard I try to keep them happy," said one supervisor, "somebody in my outfit is going to be complaining. As soon as I get one problem solved, they come at me with a new one."

But the human tendency that was causing that manager so much frustration was actually his greatest asset. If his people had no needs he would have little to which to appeal. It is this very discontent—these unmet desires and impulses to want more—that makes it possible for the motivator to motivate.

As we make our transit across what Shakespeare called the ages of man, our allegiances and antipathies continue to change. What motivates one's child this year may be quite ineffective next year. "The only person who behaves sensibly," said George Bernard Shaw, "is my tailor. He makes new measurements every time he sees me. All the rest go on with the old measurements."

Will Individualizing Your Motivational Plan Cause You to Be Unfair?

If you fit your leadership to the individual, it might seem to invite problems. If you are more lenient with one, will not others in your group accuse you of favoritism and unfairness? Indeed they will, if you relax rules that have been announced as universal rules. There is nothing more ineffective than the boss who tries to please everyone and lets down standards for some. So favoritism will never do. Nor will it work if you try so hard to be the nice guy that you let aggressive people push you around and allow the complainers to get the most from you.

I'm not advocating favoritism, but rather individual attention to people. If you study your clients, students, or audiences carefully and tailor-make your motivational appeals, it will be seen in the long run as the *most* fair approach.

The Power of Knowing

A careful study of the people we hope to motivate has two benefits. In the first place, we can gather data with which to build our motivational appeal, and in the second place, we pay people a great compliment by devoting so much energy to knowing them. It is this second aspect to which I now wish to turn.

I once spent several months poking around library stacks and reading everything available on the subject of ecstasy. The phenomenon of peak experiences intrigued me because as a family therapist I was perplexed to understand what keeps some marriages romantic and exciting whereas others so quickly become ho-hum. In researching what Freud labeled "oceanic experiences," I discovered that one of the most important ecstasies consistently reported over the centuries is the breakthrough of knowledge—discovering the solution to a problem or bursting into some new field of learning. There appears to be great joy in the very act of knowing.

It is not by accident, then, that when the Old Testament describes the sexual experience, it frequently uses the verb "to know." When we are told that "Abraham knew Sarah," it is an eloquent and apt description of sexual love, which is both a very deep penetration and a very complete engulfing. It is, in other words, knowing another very profoundly. And in looking at happy marriages where ecstasy is preserved, it suddenly dawned on me that in such partnerships the man and woman have never stopped seeking to know one another. They do not assume that because they have lived together for 20 years they know what the other is thinking. Instead, they pay attention. They notice the changes in each other's musical tastes, vacation dreams, and goals. They are also aware of nuances of change in each other's sexual desires, and they know how to appeal to what their lover wants.

I talked to a manager of a retail store who had been having an affair outside his marriage. "Life at home has never been awful," he said, "but my wife really doesn't seem interested in what's going on with me. We've been married 26 years, and I think she assumes I'm the same guy she married 26 years ago. I bet she couldn't tell you a single book I've read in the last year, and there've probably been a dozen lying around the house. I can sit in my study at home working the computer for a five-hour stretch, and she'll never stick her head in the door and ask what I'm up to or how it's going. I've never expected passionate ecstasy with my wife at this stage, but is it expecting too much to want to be known and understood a little?''

His desires were reasonable enough. But it is always a chicken-or-the-egg question. Did his wife stop penetrating his inner psyche because she did not care, or because she'd been hurt at some point in the past, thinking that he was no longer interested in *her* life? Had he been paying attention to who she was, what she dreamed of, what she feared, what she loved? Those were the questions we pondered together, and he eventually made a very commendable decision. Regardless of who had been at fault originally, he determined that he would break off the liaison with the other woman and that he would try to end the deadlock with his wife. The way he went about the latter was very interesting. He set out to explore her as if she were a new lover whom he'd known only two weeks. The results were predictable: she now looks at him with a new intensity when he walks in the door, and their love for one another has returned.

Actor Alan Alda, who has been a very successful husband and father, says, ''The secret of living together, really, is heightening your awareness in very specific ways of what the people around you are doing. . . . See what the other people are wearing, know what your kid got in the last science test, notice if your kid wears the same clothes every day. . . . Arlene and I have always valued our marriage, so we've put a lot of energy into making it what it is.''

The principle we've been discussing in this chapter, whether it applies to loving our mates or motivating our vice-presidents, is the importance of beginning with the needs of the other person. Some think they must lead by beating their chests and saying, "Follow me, I am strong, and I know more than you." But the real leaders say, "Tell me about yourself." They know that if they listen long enough, people will *explain* how they can be motivated.

"My parents always told me that people will never know how long it takes you to do something. They will only know how well it is done."
—NANCY HANKS

"The best-kept secret in America today is that people would rather work hard for something they believe in than enjoy a pampered idleness."
—JOHN W. GARDNER

CHAPTER FOUR

A Commitment to Excellence

S o far I have been saying that the best way to bring out the best in people is to treat them in a positive, encouraging manner, capitalize on their gifts, and begin with their present needs and desires. But that does not mean that the good motivator is soft. To the contrary, most highly motivating leaders are hard as nails on standards of excellence. They hold to certain values tenaciously, and they set out to build a group of like-minded persons who share those values. A highly regarded music teacher, when asked about her unusual success with students, said, "First, I teach them that it is better to do it well than to do it badly. That may seem very rudimentary, but it is surprising how many have never been taught the pleasure and pride in setting standards and then living up to them."

Rule number three, then, for bringing out the best in people is:

---

*E*STABLISH HIGH STANDARDS FOR EXCELLENCE

The best-run companies tolerate a considerable amount of individuality, but they are also tough in enforcing certain standards. That is, the successful company has a core of beliefs which distinguishes it from many other companies. In their splendid book *In Search of Excellence*, Thomas J. Peters and Robert H. Waterman Jr. conclude that the real role of the chief executive is to manage the values of the organization. "The excellent companies," they write, "are marked by very strong cultures, so strong that you either buy into their norms or get out. There's no halfway house."

Curiously, different firms with different belief systems are able to be equally successful. At Hewlett-Packard, for example, the main premium is placed on innovation, whereas at Procter and Gamble, everyone knows that product quality is the big thing. A manager who is very successful at one company might be a complete flop at the other, but that's not the point. The essential thing is that the organization has a set of standards and that the leaders enforce rigorous adherence to them.

The same characteristic distinguishes successful families. Different families may have very different values and be equally successful. But to be a successful family there must be some concepts to which the entire family subscribes. And to build such a culture requires a tough-minded leader—not an oppressive, strong-arm leader, but one who has a certain inviolate credo and who expects high performance from everyone in the group.

Being Tough Means You Care

I know an art teacher who rotates among five different schools each week, which means that she works for five different principals. They all have different leadership styles, she says. One woman, for instance, dresses very elegantly and administers her organization with a certain amount of aloofness. She is totally professional and the school moves ahead smoothly. Another principal also has a good school, but he is much more informal. A hail-fellow-well-met type, he is loose and friendly and likes to take playground duty just for association with the kids. "But do you know what school has the *worst* morale?" this teacher asked. "It's the one where the principal tries hardest to be popular with everyone. He'll say things to us teachers like, 'Don't bother to come to the school program tonight if it's not convenient—I know you have a long drive.' Maybe he thinks the way to succeed with people is to be easy on them, but it backfires. Everybody on that staff is trying to get transferred."

Such a *laissez-faire* attitude conveys the message, "This school is not worth caring about." It is the same reason that the easy teacher and the sloppy boss are never respected—they obviously do not care either about excellence or about persons. And although we may have squirmed under hard teachers, we usually look back with gratitude to their determination that we use our potential.

The Need for Direction

The hands-off approach does not work at home any more than in the classroom or in the office. Most studies show that parents who run a tight ship and who are fairly strict produce the most secure children. The kids may complain about the rules and they may rebel, but they will grow up happier, more ambitious, and better adjusted. If you care about the members of your family, then you care about how successful they are and you devote time and energy to helping them learn to do things well. When you are overly benevolent with your children and hand out privileges and money too freely, they may give you a hug and say, "You're super." But that hug was purchased and you're not really super. You will feel a lot better about the hug you get when your kid is 25 and just got a promotion and comes to you and says, "Thanks for teaching me how to work."

"Students like to be pushed," says Bill Honig, superintendent of schools for the state of California. "Kids respect courage. They say 'If you don't make me do it, you don't care about me.' They squirm; then they do it." For all our talk about the advantages of nondirective leadership, people need to be steered. Mr. Robert S. Hughes, chairman of the board at the Robert S. Hughes Company, said to me recently, "The older I get the more I realize that our employees need more direction than we once thought." In my counseling practice, I'm now seeing lots of patients in their 20s who are wishing that their parents had given them stronger leadership. A woman said to me not long ago,

"I'm sorry mom and dad didn't give me more guidance. There are things I really need to know to function well out in the adult world, and my folks could have taught me those things. I was probably a know-it-all and didn't act as if I needed any guidance, but I did."

Leadership methods seem to vary greatly, but one constant among successful motivators is a dogged devotion to superior work. They are never namby-pambies who are easily swayed by the winds of fashion.

To be a leader you have to have some fire in your belly. When Mario Cuomo was in law school, teachers told him to change his vowel-laden last name if he wanted to get ahead in life. But Cuomo refused, for he was fiercely proud of his Italian heritage. When he ran for governor of New York in 1982, his opponent, Lewis Lehrman, spent $13.9 million—$9.6 million from his own personal fortune—compared to Cuomo's $4.8 million. At times, Cuomo was convinced that he would lose. Writing in his diary one night late in the campaign, he was tired and depressed. Looking for a pencil, he ruffled through some papers in the back of his desk drawer and turned up one of his father's old business cards. He read: "Andrea Cuomo, Italian-American Groceries—Fine Imported Products," and began to think about his father. When Andrea Cuomo arrived in America, he could not speak English and took a job digging sewer trenches. Eventually they acquired a tiny 24-hour grocery store, behind which the struggling family lived for many years.

After staring at the card, Cuomo wrote in his diary that night:

> I couldn't help wondering what Poppa would have said if I had told him I was tired or—God forbid—that I was discouraged. . . .

One scene in particular came sharply into view. We had just moved into Holliswood from behind the store. We had our own house for the first time; it even had some land around it, even trees—one in particular was a great blue spruce that must have been 40 ft. high.

Less than a week after we moved in there was a terrible storm. We came home from the store that night to find the great blue spruce pulled almost totally out of the ground and flung forward, its mighty nose bent in the asphalt of the street. When we saw our spruce defeated, its cheek on the canvas, our hearts sank. But not Poppa's.

Maybe he was 5 ft. 6 if his heels were not worn. Maybe he weighed 155 lbs. if he had had a good meal. . . . But he was stronger than Frankie and me and Marie and Momma all together.

We stood in the street looking down at the tree. The rain was falling. We waited a couple of minutes figuring things out and then he announced, "O.K., we gonna push 'im up!"

"What are you talking about Poppa? The roots are out of the ground!"

"Shut up, we gonna push 'im up, he's gonna grow again."

We didn't know what to say to him, you couldn't say no to him; not just because you were his son, but because he was so sure.

So we followed him into the house and we got what rope there was and we tied the rope around the tip of the tree that lay in the asphalt, and he stood up by the house, with me pulling on the rope and Frankie in the street in the rain, helping to push up the great blue spruce. In no time at all we had it standing up straight again!

With the rain still falling, Poppa dug away at the place where the roots were, making a muddy hole wider and wider as the tree sank lower and lower toward security. Then we shoveled mud over the roots and moved boulders to the base of the tree to keep it in place. Poppa drove stakes in the ground, tied rope from the trunk to the stakes, and maybe two hours later looked at the spruce, the crippled spruce made straight by ropes, and said, "Don't worry, he's gonna grow again."

I looked at Poppa's card from the desk and wanted to cry. If you were to drive past the house today you would see the great, straight blue spruce, maybe 65 ft. tall, pointing straight up to the heavens, pretending it never had its nose in the asphalt.

I put Poppa's card back in the drawer, closed it with a vengeance. I couldn't wait to get back into the campaign.

Cuomo went on to win the 1982 election by 180,386 votes, in large part because of his dogged determination in the face of what appeared to be insurmountable obstacles. Such determination does not come from nowhere. In this case it came from an immigrant father who had fire in his belly and who thought it important to give strong direction to his family.

The Art of the Reprimand

If we are going to enforce high standards it will require us to tell people when they do not meet those standards. In their little book *The One Minute Manager*, Kenneth Blanchard and Spencer Johnson advocate giving "one-minute reprimands."

One of the surest signs of a weak manager or a poor parent is the fear of telling people in your organization when they have erred. Here are some simple suggestions for handing out a reprimand:

1. Do it immediately.

2. Before going further, confirm the facts. Be sure your information is correct.
3. Be very specific in telling them what is wrong. Try to criticize their behavior, not their motives.
4. Show your feelings: anger, annoyance, frustration.

Some of us may want to disagree with Blanchard and Johnson on the amount of time necessary for a reprimand; most employees or children will require more than 60 seconds before the matter is fully discussed. But the point is still well taken—we will never be able to manage and motivate if we are afraid to correct people's mistakes. We may arouse the occasional ire of people and we may even be called ruthless by some. But what has actually happened is that we've made it clear that we will not sanction incompetence. "The dream begins," says Dan Rather, "with a teacher who believes in you, who tugs and pushes and leads you on to the next plateau, sometimes poking you with a sharp stick called truth."

When Motivators Are Unpopular

If you hand out reprimands, you must be willing to allow the other person to be quite unhappy with you for a time. To be an inspiring leader you do not have to be the smartest, or even the hardest-working person in the group. What it does require is that you be firm—firm in your dedication to excellence, even if it makes you temporarily unpopular. Leadership doesn't mean winning popularity contests. "Some of the most talented people are terrible leaders because they have a crippling need to be loved by everyone," says James Schorr of Holiday Inns. Coach Lombardi's philosophy was this: "I hold it more important to have the players' confidence than their affection." And child psychologist Haim Ginott said, "A good parent must like his children, but he must not have an urgent need to be liked by them every minute of the day."

Handling Discipline with Ingenuity

One of the best persuaders and motivators of all time was Anne Sullivan, the teacher who led Helen Keller out of her frightening world of silence and darkness. When Miss Sullivan arrived in Tuscumbia, Alabama, she found a young, undisciplined animal. By this time one or two people had already told Helen's mother that her daughter was an idiot, and with her mind chained in darkness, her growing body was indeed governed by animal impulses. Then one day at the waterpump, Miss Sullivan broke through as Helen connected the sensation of the gushing water from the spout with the finger-spelling Anne was doing on the other palm: w-a-t-e-r. "Caught up in the first joy I had known since my illness," Keller wrote, "I reached out eagerly to Annie's ever-ready hand, begging for new words to identify whatever objects I touched. Spark after spark of meaning flew from hand to hand and, miraculously, affection was born."

Most of the world knows the spine-tingling story of how, with Miss Sullivan's help, Helen Keller went on to be an international heroine and a pathfinder for many handicapped persons. But it is not as commonly remarked that Miss Sullivan was very tough with her pupil throughout those years. The young animal did not suddenly become a subdued and cooperative child simply because she could now communicate with others; it came because Miss Sullivan was a tough disciplinarian and made the same demands for her behavior that she would have expected of a seeing and hearing child. "As soon as I had enough words to distinguish between right and wrong," wrote Keller, "she put me to bed whenever I committed a misdeed. Laziness, carelessness, untidiness, and self-justification were faults that she combatted with ingenuity, humor, and lightning sarcasm."

The Power of a Challenge

People are never inspired by a job or a family where nothing is asked of them. They are inspired by challenges. Charles de Gaulle, who knew a great deal about activating a nation, said, "A man of character finds a special attractiveness in difficulty, since it is only by coming to grips with difficulty that he can realize his potentialities." And it was William James who said, "Need and struggle are what excite and inspire us."

When Jesus called his disciples, he did not call them to ease and comfort. Instead he called them to take up their crosses and follow him, he told them the way would be narrow and hard, and he summoned them to sacrifice. Why would anyone be willing to join a movement that included such danger and hardship? Because such a challenge possesses an appeal that is universal. Garibaldi recruited the army with which he liberated Italy by calling for such as were ready to accept cold, hunger, nakedness, and death. When Mother Teresa of Calcutta accepts a new young girl into the Missionaries of Charity she is not nearly so gentle with them as we might expect. The rule is that she must go to the Home of the Dying the very next day and begin. Sister Bernard, one of the original 12 who began with Mother Teresa, says of the early days of the order, "It was tough. And she wanted it to be tough. She didn't want to make it easy."

The Lure of a Cause

Such demanding leadership is always the most compelling and the most successful, in part because people long for a cause. Sybil Ferguson, a homemaker in the community of Rexburg, Idaho (population 11,000), discovered some effective methods of losing weight and her friends began complimenting her on her new good looks and asking for help in doing the same. The result was the first Diet Center, in Rexburg. That was in 1970. Now there are more than 1900 Diet Centers around the world, grossing $90 million a year, and a new one opens somewhere every day. Sybil Ferguson and her husband still operate the company from Rexburg. What accounts for such success? In part it is because she has emphasized from the beginning that they are far more than a company—they are a movement, a cause. One of Mrs. Ferguson's assistants says, "People here feel a part of the cause to which we are all dedicated—helping overweight people overcome their problem—and this is seen as much more than a job."

When the 23rd Olympic Games came to the United States, the doomsayers predicted a disaster. In everyone's minds were the terrorist attacks which made Munich a tragedy and the fiscal disaster in Montreal which left the government $1 billion in debt.

But the U.S. games proved to be a smashing success, in large part due to Peter Ueberroth, the 42-year-old optimist who masterminded the triumph and turned in a surplus of more than $200 million. Of Ueberroth's mind-set, Robert Ajemian wrote in *Time*: "He has a way of turning whatever he touches into a cause. To be involved in difficult problems with difficult goals lifts him up."

Ueberroth made speech after speech to the 72,000 Olympic workers (about half of them volunteers) about how together they had to climb a majestic mountain. Such language might sound corny to some, but there was no question in anyone's mind that Ueberroth saw it exactly that way. Such commitment to the cause could also make him imperious with those whose dedication did not seem adequate. One day in the headquarters cafeteria he stopped to talk to some employees who were having lunch. The chat was pleasantly routine until one of the women asked about possible salary increases. Ueberroth, the unsalaried volunteer, turned cold and snapped: "You shouldn't be working here if you don't understand what we are trying to do."

There is no substitute for the motivating power of a great cause. It is a canard of our culture that we would be happier if we weren't so busy, if we weren't working so hard, if we didn't have so much homework. If only we could relax more and take more vacations. But leisure has little to do with one's happiness. To the contrary, I've found that the happiest people have found some cause and they stride through life propelled by a commitment. The fact of the matter is that most people are bored. When students dislike school it is often because school expects so little of them. When people hate their jobs it is rarely because their jobs ask

66

too much of them—it is because their jobs are routine and humdrum. So if a leader appears on the horizon who has high standards for performance and who will offer them a challenge and a cause, they will be more likely to follow.

Realistic Expectations

Before leaving this topic of excellence and commitment, we must add a warning about going overboard in urging people to shoot for the stars. It is possible, of course, to ask so much that we intimidate people and cause them to give up. No one can work indefinitely at something without having some success. David C. McClelland, a psychologist at Harvard University, has done extensive research on what he terms "achievement motivation" and has found that the best-motivated people like to have clear-cut objectives before them, but objectives that are attainable. When a group of business people are placed in an experimental group and invited to devise games with spikes and a handful of rope rings, some people will stand quite close, easily ringing the spike—and quickly lose interest. Others will stand relatively far away, fail to make any ringers, and become discouraged. But the people who predictably will be most successful in business will stand just far enough away to make the toss challenging, yet not so far away as to make success impossible. McClelland has learned that these people will stay consistently motivated, and they are hooked on what he calls "accomplishment feedback"—a continuous sense of satisfaction in their ability to meet short-run goals. In other words, they want to have their capacities stretched, but they need to have regular successes. There is an important lesson to be learned here by all leaders and teachers: in pressing for excellence, we must be careful to have goals that are both challenging and realistic, and we must devise a graded progression of objectives, so that our people can enjoy the regular feedback of success.

Track coach Dean Cromwell would say, "Optimism is most helpful when it is really convincing. So aim for a reasonable goal. I tell a boy to try to be sixth if I know he can do no better. If your friend is second assistant bottle-washer today, don't tell him that he can be company president tomorrow. If he doesn't believe you, it will do no good. Get him working furiously to become top bottle-washer. If your son got a D on the last history test, tell him you're betting he'll make a C on the next."

In the following chapter I will make some suggestions on how to cope with outright failure in the people you lead.

CHAPTER FIVE

The Management
of Failure

In late May 1940, the English army faced on the beaches of Dunkirk what could be its most ignominious defeat. The German Panzer divisions had pushed the ill-equipped and ill-trained British forces into a tighter and tighter huddle, and Hitler was ready to jerk the noose already around their neck. The only escape was the sea. But now the advantage of being a seafaring people came to the rescue. The brunt of the Dunkirk evacuation was borne by the navy, but everybody else who had a boat joined in. Fishing trawlers and drifters, tugs and motorboats, yachts and pleasure boats, old Thames steamers and river craft of every kind joined into a great armada in reverse to pluck the beleaguered British troops out of Hitler's clutches. The waters on the Dunkirk beaches were like a boiling inferno, but again and again the little boats plunged in and brought back load after load of troops.

One third of them were lost, but the bulk of the army was saved. And the British spirit was still intact. A. L. Rowse tells what it was like, seeing the troops coming back: "We remember them as they came back from the Channel and passed through the ports and railway

stations, where civilians brought them food and cig-
arettes—blackened, dirty, disarmed, but not at all dis-
mayed by their ordeal.''

All their equipment had been abandoned in France—
artillery, machine guns, automobiles, thousands of ri-
fles. It would take years to train and equip an army
capable of reentering Europe. In Churchill's report to
the nation that week, he did not assign to Dunkirk any
of the attributes of victory. But he did say, ''We shall
go on to the end, we shall fight in France, we shall
fight in the seas and oceans . . . we shall defend our
island, whatever the cost may be, we shall fight on
the beaches, we shall fight on the landing grounds, we
shall fight in the fields and in the streets . . . we shall
never surrender.''

Anyone desiring to be a good leader must learn the
art of helping people rekindle their will after such an
episode. In fact, it perhaps can be said that no one will
ever be an effective motivator who does not know how
to help people with their failures.

The different ways in which different people react
to failure is a motivational puzzle. What is it that causes
some to sail forth into the world with great promise
and a strong trajectory, then quit after only one defeat?
Unable to rise from their failure, they scale down their
dreams and live out their lives in resignation and cau-
tious mediocrity. On the other hand, what causes some
to be capable of endless renewal? Failure seems only
to make them more determined to overcome, and when
they stumble, they pick themselves up, look around to
learn from their mistakes, and then go on to finish the
race with distinction.

If leaders can teach people how to handle failure
creatively, it may be the most important contribution

they can make. So rule number four for bringing out the best in people is this:

CREATE AN ENVIRONMENT WHERE FAILURE IS NOT FATAL

I talked once to a woman with vast experience in politics who had observed the great and the near great. She said, "Do you know what separates achievers from the masses? I once thought it was drive, intelligence, connections. But the longer I've watched people, the more I've discovered that, paradoxically, it is an ability to fail that makes for lasting success."

That lesson was learned early by a young black girl who made her debut at New York's Town Hall too early. She was not ready for Town Hall, either in experience or personal maturity, and the critics flayed her. She went home to Philadelphia in disgrace. The members of her church had started her on her career by pooling their pennies, nickels, and dimes for what they called "The Fund for Marian Anderson's Future," and after the New York debacle, she could not face her old friends or her teachers.

The singer's embarrassment and depression lasted for more than a year, but Marian Anderson's mother would not give up. She continued to encourage her, to tell her that failure is only temporary, to try to convince her that she still had a gift. Then one afternoon one of her pep talks sank in. She said, "Marian, grace must come before greatness. Why don't you think about this failure a little and pray about it a lot?" Looking back, the great vocalist (who went on to help many other singers survive the despair she felt in that first bitter defeat) said, "Whatever is in my voice, faith has put there. Faith and my mother's words: 'Grace must come before greatness.' "

It is a wise mother and a wise leader who tenaciously teaches people how to learn from their mistakes and how to keep from quitting. Some business people are constantly firing employees who stumble, for they cannot brook failure. But the best managers expect their people to make mistakes, and instead of replacing staff constantly, they recognize that it is more efficient to teach people how to cope with their failures and learn from their mistakes. In other words they are not so much judges and disciplinarians as they are coaches and teachers, and they know that when people fall it is one of the most important intersections for their motivational work. If they can impart perseverance and tenacity and help others learn from their errors, they will be doing them an important service and at the same time be creating a superior organization.

When asked for the ingredients of good management, Charles Knight, chief executive officer of Emerson Electric, said boldly, "You need the ability to fail. I'm amazed at the number of organizations that set up an environment where they do not permit their people to be wrong. You cannot innovate unless you are willing to accept some mistakes."

When the Motivator Shows How to Fail by Example

But how do we instill these attitudes in our group? One way is by personal example. Some people carry the mistaken notion that to lead well one must have a string of unadulterated successes. So they go to great lengths to hide their failures. But in fact, a reputation for being a tenacious gambler, for having lost a few battles, undaunted, is probably more inspiring than anything.

We must dispel from our minds the idea that strong people never fail. Richard J. Needham says, "Strong people make as many and as ghastly mistakes as weak people. The difference is that strong people admit them, laugh at them, learn from them. That is how they become strong."

If you want to convince your group of that, the best way is to let them see you failing. You can be very sure that the people under you are going to be watching very closely to see how you react when you stumble. If you try to pretend that it was not a failure, or ignore it, or become more cynical and less of a dreamer for the failure, that lesson, too, will not be lost on them.

Helping Your People Handle Rejection

One of the most critical motivational contributions leaders can make is in the help they offer their followers who come back from rejection. Such a situation will occur in a family when your child crawls home after losing a class election; it will occur in a marriage when your mate loses an important promotion; and it will happen when a salesperson comes in to the home office after a month of disappointing results.

The wise leader does everything possible to provide refueling for those who have been to the front and return in a battered condition. Tom Keegan, who worked his way up to become sales manager for a large carpet company, says, "I was on the road for years and now that I'm a manager, I'm determined not to forget how lonely it gets out there. When you're in your car going from one account to another and everyone is telling you that your prices are too high and your company stinks, the last thing in the world you need is to feel that your manager is against you too. You've got to know that the company is on your side."

That is equally important in the family. Home should be a refuge where you can get your wounds bandaged and where people accept you no matter how you have stumbled on the outside. The knowledge that you have such a secure place can keep a person going for a long time in a very hostile environment.

The refuge concept, like all good things, can be carried too far, until an employee or a child is coddled and protected from his or her failings. Then the person becomes overly defensive, blaming everything on outside forces. Dr. Robert N. McMurray, a consulting psychologist, surveyed 220 men who were able-bodied, of above-average intelligence, and seemingly well-trained, yet who could not hold a job or make a success of any relationship for very long. He classified them as half-failures, and the major reason, he found, was that they could not face up to any kind of shortcoming. In childhood they had been protected from the consequences of their own mistakes by indulgent parents. When they failed in school, their teacher was blamed. When they couldn't get along at work, it was office politics. This is what Thomas Carlyle called the greatest of all faults—to be conscious of none.

How to Correct Errors without Defeating Enthusiasm

What then is the balance between keeping high standards and nurturing followers when they do not meet those standards? Parents and managers have the identical problem: how to expect high performance and still tolerate failure. The fatal mistake made by some is to lash out so harshly at young people for some failure that they scale down their aspirations and no longer strive for high goals. It was Seneca who said, "If thou art a man, admire those who attempt great things, even though they fail," and Theodore Roosevelt said, "The only man who never makes a mistake is the man who never does anything." We should probably reprimand our group if they are *not* having a few flops, for if they're not failing now and again it's a sign they're playing it safe.

"Failure never hurt anybody," Jack Lemmon once said. "It's the fear of failure that kills you, that kills artists. You've got to go down that alley and take those chances." Effective motivators keep a bag of tricks with them and use whatever devices are necessary to help their followers stare down failure, learn from their mistakes, and go on with perseverance. At times you yell them on and persuade them to run one more lap when they're convinced they can't take another step. At other times you push them back on the horse that has thrown them, before fear has time to take over. In some cases you rearrange duties so that their string of failures can be interrupted and they can have some small successes. In other words, the motivator knows that the fear of failure can destroy a dreamer with fine prospects and that the most important lesson they can learn is that failures are only the whetstones of life.

Imagine, for instance, how easy it would have been for this young man to have bowed his head and given up. He failed in business in '31, he was defeated for the legislature in '32, he was elected to the legislature in '34. His sweetheart died in '35, he had a nervous breakdown in '36, he was defeated for speaker in '38, he was defeated for elector in '40, he was defeated for Congress in '43, he was elected to Congress in '46, defeated for Congress in '48, defeated for Senate in '50, defeated for vice president in '56 and for Senate in '58. But fortunately he was elected president in 1860. His name was Abraham Lincoln.

Where did Lincoln learn such tenacity and such an ability to be undeterred by failure? Much of it came from within, of course—that character which Sandburg called a combination of velvet and steel. But he also persevered because some people believed in him, encouraged him when he despaired, taught him that failure was not permanent, and pushed him on. Perhaps there were other Lincolns born on the western frontier in that century, but for the want of such teachers and friends, they now lie in obscure graves.

> *"I have found the best way to give advice to your children is to find out what they want and then advise them to do it."*
> —HARRY TRUMAN

CHAPTER SIX

Building Inner Drive

John Lubbock once remarked that it is important not so much that every child should be taught as that every child should be given the wish to learn. I've never met a teacher who would disagree with that, but here's the rub. How do we go about instilling such a desire for learning? When educators get together and talk about motivation, it is their most frequent question. How can we encourage internal drive, instead of depending on external stimulation?

The same problem of internal versus external motivation exists for supervisors of all kinds, of course. Since we cannot be with people all the time, using incentives, threats, pep talks, and all the other tricks in our bag, the ultimate test of our motivational power will be how well they perform when we're not there.

Mrs. Cherry Henricks, who is a highly successful entrepreneur and interior designer—and whose firm has outgrown its offices three times in the past three years—helped give me the answer to this question. When I asked her if she thought motivation had to come from other people or if it could be generated from within, she replied, "It takes both, obviously, and I'm terribly dependent on my partners for inspiration, but I think I can motivate myself quite well with a very simple technique—by setting goals for myself. If I write them down, and get them very, very specific, that really gets me going."

The more I thought about Henricks's comment, the more I realized the wisdom in what she said. Internal drive can best be developed by encouraging people to probe within themselves until they find specific goals and dreams. Then we help them stay with their self-prescribed plan. Some people have the idea that the best motivators are the people with the most glib and forceful tongues, who by the power of their personalities are able to get lots of followers behind their projects. Such leaders go at their work as if subordinates had to be pushed and persuaded and cajoled to climb aboard their bandwagons. But the smart motivator knows that people have certain beliefs and causes to which they are already committed and certain directions in which they are already going. In other words, they have their own bandwagons.

What I'm recommending here is quite opposite from the foolish remark, "You've got to plant your idea in people's heads, then convince them that it was *their* idea in the first place." That is the sort of manipulation that eventually backfires, and it should be avoided at all costs. On the other hand, if we fish long enough we will find good ideas coming from other people which we can legitimately support.

So rule number five for bringing out the best in people is this:

---

*I*F THEY ARE GOING ANYWHERE NEAR WHERE YOU WANT TO GO, CLIMB ON OTHER PEOPLE'S BANDWAGONS

When one looks at certain famous families, it is puzzling that some children turn out to be so much more successful than others. Why, for instance, did Joseph Kennedy's sons excel while Franklin Roosevelt's did not? Certainly FDR had as good an understanding of power and how to use it as did Joe Kennedy. Part of the answer to that riddle may be found in Franklin Roosevelt Jr.'s remark that an appointment was always required if he wanted to see his father. One day, when the boy had a pressing problem, FDR listened to his son but never stopped working at his desk. When the boy stopped talking, FDR said absently, "Glad you could drop by," and the interview was over. Contrast that with Joe Kennedy's ferocious interest in his children's lives. For all his shortcomings, Kennedy's loyalty to his children was absolute. "My business is my family and my family is my business," he said. John F. Kennedy once told Steve Smith, "You know, when I was just trying out for the freshman team for some of those swimming meets, my dad was always there. He was *always* there. He did the same for all the kids."

A father who will encourage his children in pursuing as many of their goals as possible, and who will get on his kids' bandwagons in such a fashion can make a crucial difference in their lives.

Inspiring Change

In this book we are discussing what is really a very dangerous undertaking: how to help people change. Most people are very suspicious of us if we enter their lives with the intent of changing them, for most reformers have a certain air of superiority—they think they know how their children or their employees need to shape up, and in almost every instance people resist such reformers.

The other extreme is to profess no aspirations to change people and to talk in very pious language about "accepting" everybody. Many psychotherapists, for instance, say that they have no desire to reform their patients and claim to stay nonjudgmental, nondirective, and permissive in their approach to clients. Yet that, also, is unrealistic. When such therapists talk shop with other professionals, it is obvious that they have very strong opinions about how their patients need to change. They are angry about the man who won't stop drinking, the woman who is abusive with her children, the husband who is playing mind games on his wife.

Influencing without Intimidating

Most of us *do* want to change such people. But how can we motivate them to change without manipulating or bullying them? How can one be a helping, inspiring leader and still leave people free? These are not easy questions, and we will be returning to them in several other contexts. But for now, let me offer a simple model that comes out of my practice of psychotherapy.

If I tried to decide how each new patient needed to change in order to be happy, I would be inviting a psychotic break of my own, for that would be playing God. Rather, my goals are much more modest. I see myself primarily as a clarifier, and when patients enter treatment they must assume a lot of responsibility for their therapy. So in our early sessions I ask questions such as these:

- How would you like to change?
- What would it take to make you happy?
- In what ways do you want to modify your behavior?

In other words, I'm asking them to set the goals for our work together. Then when I understand their aims, I'll do everything possible to help them reach those goals. A patient might, I suppose, present objectives with which I could not in good conscience cooperate. But that has never happened. People often need our help in probing their inner needs and determining what they really want in life, but once they begin to articulate their goals, they are often quite similar to the ones I would have suggested.

So I'm glad I remained silent. And now we're on a different footing together. I'm not there as a reformer, but as one helping them in their own plan of self-improvement. I've joined *their* bandwagon.

Managers and teachers, of course, are less free to let people set their own objectives than the psychotherapist. There are machines to build, calls to make, or things to learn, and if our employees and students have other goals, our first response is to tell them they'll have to subordinate them.

But when you are tempted to give such a knee-jerk response, remember a technique used by Paul "Bear" Bryant, the coach who won 323 college football games—more than anyone in history. Perhaps there is no field, except the military, where one is asked to subordinate personal goals more completely than in football. There the coach supposedly has clear-cut objectives, and the task of the team is to fall in line. But at the beginning of each season at Alabama, Bryant had every member of his squad write out personal goals for the year, and only after reading those did Bryant design a set of objectives for the team. When he asked their goals he was conveying at least a threefold message: (1) I care about you and what you want; (2) you should be thinking ahead; and (3) we are building a team in which we are hoping everyone can pursue their goals, and I'm going to incorporate into our general plan as many ways as possible for you to reach yours.

One reason some parents are at constant loggerheads with their sons and daughters is that the children's goals and the parents' goals seem so different. This will always be a part of the parent-child deadlock, but some parents compound the problem by failing to do what Bryant did—they do not even inquire into their child's current dreams. If they were to ask, they might discover some bandwagons they could gladly help push.

Can parents really do much to encourage self-reliance? "Yes they can," says Ruth Stafford Peale:

The secret is this: watch to see where a child's innate skills or talents lie, then gently. . . lead or coax him or her in those areas. It may be difficult for a father who was a crack athlete to understand a son who would rather play chess than football. But chess, not football, is what such a boy needs if confidence is to grow in him. If he does one thing well he will come to believe that he can do other things well.

I'm eager not to be misunderstood at this point. I'm not saying that we should be weak leaders who allow others to set the goals for our group, with the result that the organization lurches about ineffectively. People want strong leaders with clear objectives. Bryant is a good illustration of this kind of leader. But the best coaches and best managers also encourage personal goals and do everything possible to help their people get where *they* want to go.

The Consistency Principle

There may have been another reason Bryant had his players put their goals in writing: once people have committed themselves to objectives, a number of psychological influences begin to take effect which greatly increase the odds that they will achieve those goals. Deep within us, directing our actions with a quiet power, is an almost obsessive desire to be and appear to be consistent with what we have already done. In every group, inconsistency is deplored and consistency is valued. This is as true among prison inmates as it is among church members. Anyone whose opinions can be easily influenced is thought of as indecisive, weak-willed, and scatterbrained.

Dr. Leon Festinger, the pioneer researcher in this field (called Cognitive-Dissonance Theory), says that inner dissonance, or the fear that we are inconsistent, has the same energizing properties as hunger or frustration. Therefore, once we have made a choice or taken a stand, we will crash through enormous obstacles to behave consistently with that position. And we will also adjust our thinking radically to make it consistent with our actions. Let's take, for example, a man who is being sexually faithful to his wife. He will usually hold strong convictions about marital fidelity. One naturally says, "Of course. That's the reason he's faithful—because of what he believes." But not always. Notice what happens if he starts cheating on her. Now he will come up with all sorts of rationalizations to justify his behavior, and his beliefs seem to change very radically, which is to say that often our attitudes follow behavior rather than causing it.

Social scientists Jonathan Freedman and Scott Fraser have reported an astonishing experiment in which a researcher, posing as a volunteer worker, went door to door in a California neighborhood, making a preposterous request of homeowners. They were asked to allow a large, ugly public-service billboard to be set on their front lawn which declared "Drive Carefully." The great majority (83%), of course, refused. But then the researchers used a slightly different approach with another group of people and got over half to agree.

The grounds for this compliance was something that had happened to the homeowners two weeks earlier: they had made a small commitment to promote driver safety. A different volunteer had come to their doors and asked them to accept and display a small three-inch-square sign that read, "Be a Safe Driver." It was such a trifling request that nearly everyone agreed to do it. But the effects of the agreement were enormous, because when the other volunteer came and asked them to display the large billboard, most of them were now ready to do so.

A Change in Self-Perception

How can we explain this? We can understand some of it by looking at the importance of self-image. When the people put up the first message, they began to view themselves differently. They were observing their own behavior just as everyone else would, and they saw themselves as persons concerned about safety, people who cooperated in good causes. So it seemed consistent with this for them to be agreeable about the large billboard. The same thing is at work when people go public with any belief or plan: they will then channel an enormous amount of energy into living up to those commitments.

It now becomes more apparent why successful religious groups urge their converts to make some public testimony to their faith, and why effective motivators do everything they can to get the other person to state clear-cut, specific objectives. Sales trainer Tom Hopkins says that the best way to convince a man of something we know to be true is not to ram the facts down his throat or to tell him how stupid we think he is because he won't admit the truth of our statements. "The professional salesperson operates on a different concept," says Hopkins, "one that's simple and effective. Here it is: 'If I say it, they can doubt me; If they say it, it's true.' "

We must avoid several explosive mines in this field. In the first place, the consistency principle can be used to manipulate people into doing things quite contrary to their own best interests. Unscrupulous salespeople or demagogues like Jim Jones have been able to persuade persons to do demonic things with the consistency principle. First they get a small commitment from someone. Then they ask for increasingly extreme actions, all in the name of consistency. We must be careful to arrange for space in our relationships and allow people either to change their minds or to say, "This is as far as I want to go."

Dangerous Self-Concepts

There is another thing that warrants caution. It is very dangerous to allow people to declare themselves publicly on negative aspects of themselves. If a man regards himself as someone who follows the philosophy, "I never get mad, I just get even," or if a girl thinks, "I'm terrible at math," we must avoid situations where they might state that too firmly. If a girl tells her whole class that she is "terrible at math," great harm has been done, for she will go to remarkable lengths to prove herself right. And the man who thinks of himself as vindictive will be more and more set in such behavior the more frequently he describes himself that way.

A. W. Combs has written a sentence which should be taped to the bathroom mirrors of all parents and executives, to be read five times every morning before entering the world. The sentence is this: "The maintenance and enhancement of the perceived self are the motives behind all behavior." If the children we see at breakfast or the employees we greet upon arriving at the office perceive of themselves in certain negative ways, then they will act in ways to be consistent with that image. So our task is far deeper than changing the outward behavior: we must get to the self-concept. And especially with teenagers, the self-concept with which we are working may be very poor. Child psychologist James Dobson writes, "I have observed that the vast majority of those between 12 and 20 years of age are bitterly disappointed with who they are and what they represent. In a world that worships superstars and miracle men, they look in the mirror for signs of greatness, seeing only a terminal case of acne."

Negative self-perceptions should be treated with benign neglect, and we should reflect back any positive perceptions of who they are. When students think of themselves as poor at math, what they may mean is that they had a hard time in their last math class, and our task is to reinforce all evidence that they are more gifted than it seemed. As S. I. Hayakawa writes, there is a vast difference between saying, "I have failed three times," and saying, "I am a failure."

Specificity

Not only do we want people to go public with their goals and dreams; we also want them to be very specific about what they want. Dr. Neil Clark Warren and I have for several years offered intensive weekend seminars on the subject, "Self-Esteem and the Discovery of Joy." During the weekend we ask participants to write for 20 minutes on this question: "If money were no object and you could have exactly the sort of life you would like, what would it be?" The papers come back with strangely vague and ill-defined answers. It is obvious that many of these persons have never given themselves the freedom to dream concretely; consequently they have achieved little concrete happiness.

"You'd better know what you want, because you'll probably get it," says Dan Greenburg, and indeed there is an almost bewitching way in which our success in life is dependent on our ability to set very high and very specific goals. The legendary industrialist, Henry Kaiser, when asked to give his philosophy of success, said, "Decide what you want most of all out of life; then write down your goals and a plan to reach them."

The more I counsel people, the more I'm aware that most people are very different from Kaiser in that respect. They drift along and their destinies are determined largely by the willy-nilly of circumstances. Like Mr. Micawber, they're always hoping that something will turn up, but good things don't usually "turn up" for us any more than they did for Mr. Micawber.

There is simply great power in setting goals for ourselves. I talked to a real estate salesman who had normally made about $40,000 a year in sales commissions. Then one year his income shot up to $95,000. I asked him why. "Simple," he said. "My wife was seriously ill and in the hospital much of that year, and I knew exactly how much money I had to make to provide for her care. That's what I made, almost to the penny." When we set a concrete objective and determine a definite road map for getting there, it can be transformational.

The Power of Dreams

A father I know says, "My parents never talked to me about college. In fact, they never talked to me much about *anything* ahead. They only seemed to live in the present. My daughter is only 13, but we're always discussing where she might like to go to school and what she'd like to major in. I know better than to force her into making any decisions this early, and she'll probably change her mind a dozen times, but I don't care. The important thing is that we both have fun dreaming about the future.''

That girl is very fortunate to have such a future-oriented parent, for without in any way manipulating her, he is encouraging her to dream. Anyone can puncture people's dreams and tell them they're unrealistic, but it takes an unusual person to know the value of planning big, shooting high, and keeping the upward look.

The best leaders are more than optimists (though almost every good motivator is a strong positive thinker). They are also futurists. That is, they love to live in the future, dream about the future, talk about the future—and they are always urging people around them to do the same.

Management by Encouragement

Scudder N. Parker once said, "People have a way of becoming what you encourage them to be—not what you nag them to be." It is a very basic human need—the need to have someone encourage us and spur us on to higher things. A client, who is now a famous surgeon, says that he believes in "management by encouragement," and goes on to explain what he means by that. "When I was in high school in Iowa, I had a swim coach whom I remember vividly. He was always yelling at us. But he was not yelling to bawl us out. He would yell things like, 'C'mon, Johnson, get the lead out! Faster! You can do it!' and that was what I needed. In fact, I guess I owe much of my success to that coach, because when I'm standing at the operating table, I can still hear him shouting at me. So I've always tried to be a similar encouragement to the people under me. I may be hard on them, and expect a lot, but what I'm basically yelling is, 'C'mon, you can do it.' "

In 1875, a sickly child was born in Upper Alsace who was slow to read and write and was a poor scholar. But as he grew up he made himself master subjects that were particularly difficult, such as Hebrew. In music, he turned out to be a genuine prodigy, playing the organ at eight when his legs were scarcely long enough to reach the pedals. At nine he substituted for the regular organist in a church service.

His name was Albert Schweitzer, and everyone knows how by early manhood he had several professional lives proceeding concurrently. At the University of Strasbourg he earned his first Ph.D. in philosophy, then went on to win doctorates in theology and music theory. By the time he was 30, he had a flourishing career as a concert organist and was publishing a stream of books. But then he abruptly stopped his academic career in order to study medicine and devote the rest of his life to being a missionary. This had begun when by chance he read a magazine article about the Congo. "While we are preaching to these people about religion," the article said, "they are suffering and dying before our eyes from physical maladies."

Schweitzer had received his calling, and he began to lay plans to go to Africa. Friends protested: if the aborigines of Africa needed help, let Schweitzer raise money for their assistance. He certainly was not called upon to wash lepers with his own hands.

There will always be such people who try to tell us to be realistic, people who seem to find it their calling to attempt to flatten our dreams and diminish our lives. But there will always be a few, thankfully, who will encourage our ideals and gladly join us in our goals. When Schweitzer fell in love with Helen Bresslau, the daughter of a Jewish historian, he bluntly proposed: "I am studying to be a doctor for the Negroes of Africa. Would you spend the rest of your life with me—in the jungle?"

And she answered, "I shall become a nurse. Then how could you go without me?" And on Good Friday of 1913, the two of them left for French Equatorial Africa. For more than 50 years he served there, eventually to become a Nobel laureate and a legend.

We may not always be able to adjust the course of our lives to make our goals correspond exactly to the goals of the people around us, as did Helen Schweitzer, for our road maps must at times be different from theirs. But our rule still stands: If they are going anywhere near where you want to go, climb on other people's bandwagons.

> *"Example is the school of mankind, and they will learn at no other."*
> —EDMUND BURKE

CHAPTER SEVEN

The Power of the Success Story

A t an insurance convention in Atlanta some time ago, I shared the speakers' platform with Mr. Lee Iacocca, chairman of the board at Chrysler Corporation. The auto industry was in a slump at that time, and no one was sure if Chrysler would survive. Mr. Iacocca's address was entitled, "So You Think *You've* Got Troubles!" He talked for 60 minutes, and it was a stirring speech. Frequently interrupted by applause, he related how Chrysler had cut their white collar staff from 40,000 to 20,000 and yet was producing more cars than at any time in the last three years. And finally they were making a modest profit again. It was a rags-to-riches story on a corporate scale.

I returned to my hotel strangely stirred and energized. My work is not at all similar to Mr. Iacocca's. He is head of a large automaker in Detroit and I am a psychotherapist and writer in Los Angeles. Yet Mr. Iacocca's story of success made me feel like attacking my work with renewed zest and dedication.

An important psychological principle was at work there in Atlanta: success stories have a significant ability to motivate us. So rule number six for bringing out the best in people is:

EMPLOY MODELS TO ENCOURAGE SUCCESS

Great persuaders have always been good storytellers, for they have known that we are more easily influenced by individualized examples and experiences than by general principles. Morton Hunt says that his doctor once advised him to take a certain drug for a medical problem. He asked if it was dangerous. "The doctor outlined the evidence," says Hunt, "and I felt reassured. Then he added, 'I take it myself'—and I was persuaded."

David J. Moine, a psychologist who heads his own communications training firm in Redondo Beach, California, has shown that successful salespeople use realistic examples to show the listener that another individual has made the choice he or she is being urged to make. If I'm looking at a new car and the dealer tells me about several recent customers who have purchased the car we are looking at, it pumps a certain heightened interest into the exchange.

Stories of other people convince us because they appeal to our hearts rather than our heads. They have the ability to stir our feelings powerfully and to change our attitudes. And when all is said and done, the art of motivation *is* the heightening of emotion. It is appealing to the unconscious more than the conscious, to the right side of the brain more than the left. Political scientist James MacGregor Burns, in his Pulitzer-Prize-winning book *Leadership*, comments on the uncanny power of Chairman Mao Tse-tung, whose true genius, he says, "was in understanding the emotions of others." And the best way to appeal to the emotions is by talking about people, their struggles, conflicts, and eventual triumphs.

The Bible is an emotionally stirring book, in part because it is filled with the drama of people's lives. To a large extent it is a collection of biographies of flesh-and-blood people—and its doctrines are effectively passed on in these gripping accounts. Modern journalism uses much the same approach. *The Reader's Digest, People, Guideposts*—even the famous *New Yorker* profile—all appeal to the same instinct in us: we want to know about the lives of other people.

The Legendary Hero

Most movements and organizations seem to flourish best when they have some strong figure who embodies certain principles, and from whom those principles can filter down. People such as Thomas Watson Sr. of IBM, A.P. Giannini of Bank of America, Mary Kay Ash of Mary Kay Cosmetics, or Ken Olsen of DEC take on mythic proportions. And, according to the experts on management, these legends are very important because they convey the organization's shared values or culture.

Charles Steinmetz of General Electric is a good illustration. A crippled Austrian immigrant, Steinmetz came as a young man to America and worked in Thomas Edison's laboratory. He was responsible for dozens of inventions still used by GE and other companies.

But Steinmetz is revered for other reasons. When young engineers joined the company he would invite them to his home for the weekend in order to learn what kind of people they were. Once he even adopted a GE engineer as his son and let the entire family move in with him.

Such stories, circulated through the company's informal but powerful communications network, help perpetuate GE's philosophy of fair treatment for all employees. Moreover, the specter of such leaders helps inspire excellence. A consultant working with GE was once driven past the lab where Charles Steinmetz had conducted his experiments. "Sometimes I get the feeling that I can still see the lights on in there and Steinmetz is working away," the driver said. For that man, and for other employees who never knew Steinmetz, he was still a strong influence and served as a reminder of the inventiveness that GE holds as a core value of its corporate culture.

School cultures are constructed in the same way. Coaches have always known that they could get a grip on a team by talking about some of the school's earlier athletes, like the legendary "Win one for the Gipper." Teachers would do well to use similar biography in their lectures. Telling about successful students from the past, and even bringing such graduates into class sessions, can be potent motivation. Teachers might find that their students would learn more if they occasionally forgot about covering material and instead put into their students' minds pictures of such persons as Lincoln with his books before the fireplace or Madame Curie with her instruments in the laboratory.

Families do well to inspire their younger members by continuing to keep alive the records of earlier generations. In the last three decades before she died, my grandmother devoted much of her energy to writing the stories of her buffalo-hunter father, Frank J. Brown. And she even had two books published, primarily for the benefit of the dozens of cousins and great-grandchildren. Some of us in the family thought she was unduly obsessed with these endeavors, but now that I am older I realize how much her father's life and ideals have influenced my thinking. I find myself going back to her books in order to get a better idea of who I am, and I find myself more determined than ever to carry on those traditions.

Harry Truman was once asked how he could account for his success in politics. He pointed to several pictures of family ancestors on the wall and said gruffly, "I come from good stock, and I've got a lot to live up to." There is something ennobling about being able to reach back to solid roots and imparting to our families the conviction that they are pursuing some unfinished dreams from the past.

The Contemporary Hero

In addition to the legendary heroes we have been discussing, there is another type of success story. The good motivator finds contemporary role models to hold up to the group. In fact, this is one of the most effective ways of showing employees what the boss wants done.

Let us say that Proctor and Gamble is about to face stiff competition in a certain market, and the sales manager has decided that a more aggressive approach is in order. It would be possible to send out a memo to that effect, or to make a speech on the subject at a sales meeting. But Proctor and Gamble knows that the message will be communicated far more dramatically by finding some salesman out in the field who is doing exactly what they want done, bringing him in, applauding the fellow's aggressive salesmanship, slapping him on the back, and writing him up as "salesman of the month" in the company newspaper. The obvious message is "Emulate him," and that message will come through more clearly than any memo announcing a new corporate strategy.

Looking back upon the dinner conversations with which I grew up, I now see how effectively my father used heroes to motivate his sons. A thoughtful, soft-spoken man, it would never enter his mind to lecture us about excelling or studying hard in school. But at the dinner table he *did* comment upon the people in our small town whom he admired—a businessman who was going to law school at night, or a young farmer who was taking correspondence classes. He wanted to be sure that we noticed these people. Both my brother and I went on to get doctoral degrees and, looking back, I now see how strongly our father propelled us toward success. He did what all effective managers and teachers do—he gave us strong values by holding up flesh-and-blood people who embodied those values.

"If He Can Do It, So Can You"

When our leader exposes us to successful people, it not only inculcates certain values, it also convinces us that if they can achieve, so can we. Seeing another succeed somehow inspires us to succeed. For nine years the record for the mile hovered just above four minutes. As early as 1945, Gunder Haegg had approached the barrier with a time of 4:01.4. But many people said that the limits of physical capacity had been reached and that it was impossible to break that barrier. Then in 1954 Roger Bannister broke the tape at 3:59.4. And what was the result? As soon as the myth of the "impossible barrier" was dispelled, the four-minute mile was attacked and pierced by many with apparent ease. In almost no time the four-minute achievement was bettered 66 times by 26 different men! If one dismisses this as merely the power of competition, an important motivational point will be missed. There was just as much competition before the four-minute mile was broken. What the succeeding runners discovered from Bannister was that *it could be done*. An achievement previously thought impossible was now accessible, and the concrete evidence that success was within reach inspired them on to better and better records.

If you visit a meeting of the Mary Kay organization you will see this principle applied again and again. A crowd of people will sit in rapt attention hour after hour and get more and more inspired simply by listening to success stories. The motivational technique is really quite simple. People walk up to the microphone and recount their struggles and their triumphs. The message sounds like a refrain: "If we did it, you can do it too." They show slides of their new homes and luxury cars, and they tell basically the same story: "We came from nothing. You can do the same thing simply by believing hard enough and working hard enough."

Terrence E. Deal and Allan A. Kennedy, in their splendid book *Corporate Cultures* explain the phenomenon very well:

> Heroes are symbolic figures whose deeds are out of the ordinary, but not too far out. They show—often dramatically—that the idea of success lies within human capacity.

The Optimist of Fifth Avenue

I have always wondered why some churches are successful and others are not, why some pastors are able to send their congregations away inspired and hopeful, when others seem unable to have that effect.

Many intellectuals have been less than charitable toward popularizers of religion such as Norman Vincent Peale, criticizing them for being blindly optimistic, ignoring the presence of tragedy and suffering in the world. But the longer I have sat in my counseling room and listened to people tell how they're in over their heads and sometimes feel as if they're going down for the third time, the more I've realized that no one can ignore tragedy even when they try, and that everyone needs some place to go once a week where they are picked up, given the long view, and strengthened with renewed hope.

So when I was in New York one cold December Sunday last year, I decided to go to Marble Collegiate Church and sample a sermon by the father of possibility thinking, Dr. Peale himself. People had been standing in the rain on Fifth Avenue for more than an hour to be sure of getting a seat, but no one seemed to mind. Once inside, we sang the old hymns with gusto and listened to the other ministers read from the Bible. Then, when it was time for the sermon, Dr. Peale walked slowly to the pulpit. He was 86, had been presiding there for 51 years, and the years seemed to tell. I thought to myself, *Why doesn't he retire?*

But when he reached the side of the pulpit, leaned his elbow on its top, and began to speak, I saw why his congregation wouldn't *allow* him to retire. It was as if someone had turned on a switch. He pulled himself erect, his eyes came alive, and out came a powerful sermon about worry and the spiritual principles which can help us deal with doubt. Story after story rolled out about people who had overcome their handicaps with God's help. When it was over and we filed out, all of us seemed to walk with our shoulders back and our heads held a little higher.

Later, I told Peale how touched I had been by his sermon and how I admired his technique of piling up success stories to make a point. He brushed my compliments aside with the demurrer that he did little more than "ramble" in his sermons nowadays. But then he paused a moment as he pondered the question of the stories. "Well," he said, "people used to criticize me for telling so many positive anecdotes. Come to think of it, I haven't been attacked for that in a long time. Maybe I'm slipping," he said with a twinkle. "But I try to use biographies of great people in my preaching because nothing in the Bible says we're supposed to rehearse *failure*. And the best way I know to motivate people is to show them how other men and women just like them, with similar problems to theirs, have been overcomers."

What we have been discussing in this chapter is far more than a mere modeling. What we are after is an atmosphere of enthusiasm and hope, and that can be communicated best with stories of people. David Kolb, professor of management at Case Western Reserve University, summarizes it this way: "If I see people around me succeeding, it will stimulate my desire to succeed."

In the chapter that follows I will offer some specific suggestions on helping people move from small successes to even larger ones.

"Applause is the spur of noble minds."
—C. C. COLTON

CHAPTER EIGHT

The Secret of Parlaying Small Successes into Larger Gains

When Bette Nesmith, a single parent with a nine-year old son, worked in a Dallas bank, she seemed rather average, with no particular promise for big things. She was glad to have the secretarial job—$300 a month was very good for 1951—but she did have a problem: how to correct the errors she made with her new electric typewriter. Nesmith had been a free-lance artist, and artists never correct by erasing, they simply paint over the error. So she concocted a fluid that she could use to paint over her typing errors.

Before long all the secretaries in her building were using what she then called "Mistake Out." An office supply dealer encouraged her to manufacture the paint, but marketing agencies weren't impressed, and companies (among them IBM) turned her down cold. But the secretaries continued to like the product, so Nesmith's kitchen became her first manufacturing facility. Orders began to trickle in, and she hired a college student to help sell the product. But it was not easy for two inexperienced saleswomen. "People will never paint out their mistakes," a dealer would say. Records show that from August 1959, to April 1960, the company's total income was $1,142.71, and its expenses were $1,217.35. "I don't know how I made it," Bette said. She worked part-time as a secretary, managing to buy groceries and save $200 to pay a chemist to develop a faster-drying formula.

With the improved product, Nesmith began taking her little white bottles around the country. She stopped in small towns and big cities. Upon arriving in a city, she wrote, "I'd get the phone book and write down the names of dealers and then call them. We'd go to each office supply store and leave 12 bottles." Eventually orders began to pour in and the Liquid Paper Corporation began to fly. When she sold the company in 1979, the tiny white bottles were earning $3.5 million annually on sales of $38 million, and the Gillett Co. paid $47.5 million for the firm.

The most successful people are very often like Bette Nesmith. They lead rather ordinary lives until suddenly some small success occurs. Then, unlike the average person, they parlay that small achievement to larger gains. They have what one management consultant has called "a repeater tendency." That is, once they find themselves succeeding, they set out to duplicate the accomplishment again in larger settings.

The experts at motivation encourage this snowballing of success. They study their people, looking for the strengths others have overlooked; then when small achievements begin to appear in the person's work, they know how to transform them into larger successes. The Jewish proverb is, "When luck enters, give him a seat!"

Rule number seven, then, for bringing out the best in people is one that every leader has heard in seminars and books, yet one that is widely neglected:

*R*ECOGNIZE AND APPLAUD ACHIEVEMENT

The art of praise—what is known as positive reinforcement in the current psychological jargon—is an essential art for an executive or a teacher to master. I discussed in Chapter 2 the importance of expecting the best from people, but this rule is quite different. In the earlier section I urged a positive attitude about a person's possibilities. Here I'm advocating reinforcing specific behavior. It's the difference between saying "I'm expecting great things from you" and saying "You've done a terrific job straightening out this department."

If there is a complaint employees most often express, it is this: "I never get any feedback from the boss—except when something goes wrong." And the teenagers who sit in my office tell me again and again, "My dad gets all over my case when I mess up at school, but when I bring home a good grade he acts as if it's nothing—that I'm finally doing what I should have been doing all along."

In *The One Minute Manager*, Blanchard and Johnson suggest taking frequent breaks for what they describe as "One Minute Praisings." Catch your subordinate "doing something right," they advise, then give an immediate compliment.

Such straightforward acts seem easy enough, and we all know they are an effective way of reinforcing good work in our children and employees. Yet stop and think. How long has it been since you took a full 60 seconds to talk to your son or daughter about some fine thing they've just done? Or your secretary, or the managers who work under you?

What we're discussing here is a very basic courtesy that should apply in all human relations—taking the time to thank people who help us. My friend Mike Somdal is a specialist at this. One reason he is so successful in business is that he has mastered the fine art of making people feel good by thanking them regularly. Often he will call customers simply to thank them again for the order they placed last week or for the recommendation they made to another customer or for the lunch. Anything. And before the conversation is over, Mike has often secured another order. Of course, if he called simply with ulterior motives, his clients would recognize the manipulation and resist. But Mike has made gratitude a lifelong habit, and those of us who do business with him appreciate that quality. And we respond.

Teachers are in the habit of calling parents when a student is not performing well, but they might be wise to spend a portion of that time calling parents of kids who are excelling or who have improved markedly. Such obvious respect for students gets around the school and can do a great deal to influence the climate of the classroom.

Nearly every one of us is starving to be appreciated, and when someone comes along who genuinely thanks us, we will follow that person a very long way. "The applause of a single human being," said Samuel Johnson, "is of great consequence."

The Need to Be a Winner

The old adage has it that "Nothing succeeds like success," and Peters and Waterman, in their study of the best-run companies in America, found that good organizations capitalize on that truth. They believe that if employees feel that they are doing well, they will be highly motivated. So the good companies design systems that continually reinforce the notion that their people are winners, while the not-so-excellent companies manage to keep many of their employees constantly scrambling to stay alive. IBM, for instance, sets quotas in order to make sure that 70% to 80% of its salespeople meet their goals each year, whereas at another company (an IBM competitor in part of the product line) quotas are structured in such a way that only 40% of the sales force makes them. "The systems in the excellent companies," say Peters and Waterman, "are not only designed to produce lots of winners; they are constructed to celebrate the winning once it occurs."

The Art of the Compliment

There are right ways and wrong ways of expressing appreciation and reinforcing positive behavior. Here are some suggestions for praising the people under you.

1. *Hand out commendations in public.* One-to-one praisings are not nearly as effective as public kudos. I

shall never forget a Monday afternoon during my soph-omore year in high school. I knew I had played better than usual in the previous Friday's football game, and when we assembled for practice I wondered if the coach had noticed my good blocks. Not only had he noticed! He proceeded to tell the whole *squad*. It was not bril-liant praise, for I was not a brilliant player, yet I re-member 35 years later my deep pride as he chewed out certain members of the team for poor performances and said, "Now McGinnis is another story. He's not the most coordinated player we've got, but he was really putting out on Friday." I recall the words verbatim because I desperately needed to be accepted in that group, and when the coach praised me before the team, I finally felt that I was somebody in their eyes.

Parental praisings at dinner will go further than in-dividual commendations, for you have made your child feel good before an audience. And when you have meetings with your employees, use that as an oppor-tunity to dispense your thanks. We all feign modesty and are reluctant to boast about ourselves, but I've never known people who did not like having *others* boast about them. To be present when your boss is telling about your success to someone on the telephone, for instance, or to be at a party when your wife is describing the intelligent way you handled a problem with the children yesterday—those are heady pleasures.

2. *Use every success as an excuse for celebration.* My wife is an expert at praise, and when anything out of the ordinary has happened—a book goes into another printing, or I complete a piece of furniture in the ga-rage—she makes a very big thing of it. She greets me at the door with a special hug, and perhaps with tears in her eyes, she stands with me and talks about how happy she is. Then she fixes us all a special dinner. The best families frequently celebrate each other's achievements. Life is sometimes dreary for the people around us, and we can make their existence more plea-

surable as well as increase their production if we seize every opportunity for celebration.

3. *Employ some gesture to give weight to your commendation*. One of the best investments an employer can make is to buy gifts for staff. When gift-giving becomes ritualized, as at Christmas, it never means as much as when some project is completed and you take the group to lunch and hand out tokens of your appreciation or have secretly had plaques made for their office walls. Thomas Watson Sr. at IBM is said to have made a practice of writing out a check on the spot for achievements he observed in his own peripatetic management role. When Peters and Waterman were doing the research for their book on excellence in business, they found many such examples of on-the-spot bonuses. At Foxboro Corporation, a technical advance was desperately needed for survival in the company's early days. Late one evening, a scientist rushed into the president's office with a working prototype. Dumbfounded at the elegance of the solution and bemused about how to reward it, the president bent forward in his chair, rummaged through most of the drawers in his desk, found something, leaned over the desk to the scientist, and said, "Here!" In his hand was a banana, the only reward he could immediately put his hands on. From that point on, the small "gold banana" pin has been the highest accolade for scientific achievement at Foxboro.

4. *Put your compliment in writing*. There is almost magical power in a note, especially the handwritten letter. When you are important to a person and you take the time to send a letter of commendation, that gesture can have rich rewards. Sometimes you can double the effect of the gesture by writing, not to the person, but to someone else. I have a friend who travels a great deal and when an airline employee does him a favor he not only thanks the person face to face, but

also asks for the name of the employee's supervisor, and drops a note to that supervisor when he returns home. You can be sure that carries more weight than any expression of thanks to the employee.

5. *Be very specific in your praise.* Vague slaps on the back, like telling people that they're "doing a good job" do not have nearly the impact of a detailed commendation. "I liked the way you used the colors for the tree in your picture" registers with a five-year-old more than your saying, "That's a pretty picture." It shows that you have looked at it with care. Moreover, you are reinforcing specific behavior. Let's say that your staff has successfully pulled in a large contract. They may not be aware of the exact reasons they succeeded this time and failed at another time. So it is important for you to point out exactly what you liked about their presentation, and to show that you noticed how they worked overtime on a crucial weekend to sharpen the proposal.

Karen Pryor tells about her friend Annette, who is good at comforting and offers sympathy and advice when you're in trouble. "But it is in the area of good news that Annette offers unusual reinforcement," says Pryor. "Tell her the bank approved your loan, and she does more than say, 'That's great!' She points out exactly what you did to earn and deserve the good news. 'You see?' Annette might respond. 'Remember all the trouble you went to with the phone company and getting an air-travel card? Now it pays off for you; you're recognized as a good businesswoman. But you had to make the right moves first, and you did. I'm really proud of you.' That," says Pryor, "is more than approval, that is reinforcement."

Beyond Stick and Carrot

More and more leaders are discovering that they cannot depend solely upon reward and punishment, and that they must turn to other psychological tools for inspiring top performance. In fact, according to many studies, the carrot has very limited effectiveness, and too much reward weakens motivation. As one Major League outfielder said, "I used to like playing baseball until I started getting paid for it." If people find internal reward in a task (that is, they enjoy doing it for the pleasure of the act), too much external reward (such as pay incentives for employees or candy bars for students) will weaken the internal motivation. Raymond J. Wlodkowski, of the University of Wisconsin, warns against the dangers of diminishing the task by building in too many such carrots. There is a danger, he says, of turning students into "reinforcement junkies" who must always have something extra in order to learn.

On the other hand, verbal commendation—serving notice to your students or employees that you see their work and care about its quality—has a much more powerful effect. When you praise good quality, you insure the repetition of such effort.

I have spent some time studying the techniques employed by a marketing company started less than 30 years ago and still owned by its two founders, Jay VanAndel and Rich DeVos. Last year the company grossed over a billion dollars. How has such an organization flourished so phenomenally in such a short time? There are obviously many secrets, but one of their most practiced principles (and one I see largely neglected in many less successful companies) is that they go to great lengths to celebrate the achievements of their dealers. One can scarcely do anything halfway right around the company without having it noticed and applauded. For instance, at the "Family Re-unions"—weekend affairs held in large hotel ball-rooms—a thousand dealers will gather for pep talks, seminars, and lectures. But the most important thing going on at these gatherings is the lengthy recognition ceremonies. Many gifts are handed out, and the crowd gets to its feet and cheers literally dozens of times as people are brought across the stage and their achieve-ments are announced. They are among the most clap-ping audiences I've ever addressed, and they seem to think it important to spend time applauding each other. The owners consider it important to be present at such meetings often, and Rich DeVos says, "I have one of the finest jobs in the world, because I get to spend half my time traveling around the country honoring other people."

Shaping

It is possible, of course, to overdo praise until it becomes meaningless. This is as bad as giving too many criticisms and reprimands. Let's say that you are teaching a horse to kneel on one knee. At first, during the training process, you feed the animal each time any part of the routine is done correctly. But once the habit has been established, the reward should become intermittent. Parents and executives need to remember that principle of shaping. Once good habits are estab-lished it is harmful to praise a person every time.

Another caveat is in order at this point. At times we can do harm by praising only the end result of some activity rather than the activity itself. It is possible, for example, to erode a person's love of something (such as learning) by handing out too much reward at the end. We can avoid this pitfall first by using intermittent reinforcement and second by praising people for the process as well as the product. "I admire the way you try so hard," can be worth gold to someone bogged down and unsure of success.

Finally, we must be certain—especially with children—that they feel loved for being as well as for doing. A man sat in my office sobbing uncontrollably about his marriage, which had ended primarily because he was a workaholic. He had come to me because he wanted to rid himself of this obsession with work. "But I don't want to get into my childhood," he said. "I can't stand these people who go to some head-shrinker and come out blaming everything on their parents." I agreed that there would be no benefit in blaming them, but explained that in therapy we sometimes need to probe into our childhood in order to gain some insight as to how we arrived at our present habits. The purpose is not to blame anyone but to find out how we got where we are so we can take some corrective steps to change.

He almost visibly sighed at that, and then launched into a description of his parents, who were very severe and for whom work was the highest good. "My folks never hugged us," he said, "and they thought you spoil kids by bragging on them, so my sister and I didn't get any strokes—except when we worked hard. If I mowed the lawn especially well on Saturdays, I knew that either mom would say to dad, or he would say to her, 'Didn't Harv do a good job on the lawn today?' I guess kids will do anything to get strokes if they're as hungry for them as I, so I'd go over and over that grass every Saturday, and I worked in a neighborhood store all the years I was in high school. Then when I got married I assumed that this new woman in my life would love me for working hard just like the other important woman had. But that's where I was wrong. She would have much rather had me home watching TV with her in the evenings, but somehow I could never believe that.''

That is a tragic story, and we can prevent such misconceptions in our children if we always give some affection and praise quite apart from actions. They need to know that they are valued for themselves, not merely for the degree to which they meet our expectations or follow our rules.

Observing Improvement

The alert leader will always be on the lookout for signs of positive change. There is nothing more demoralizing than to change at great expense, then have our superiors allow the change to go unnoticed. Too frequently they assume that we have the same bad habits or attitudes that we had last month, when in fact we may be quite different.

A. W. Beaven tells of a heartbreaking incident. A little girl had been misbehaving and her mother had to rebuke her often. But one day the little girl had tried especially hard and hadn't done a single thing that called for reprimand. That night, after the mother had tucked her in bed and started down the stairs, she heard her daughter sobbing. Turning back, she found her head buried in the pillow. Between sobs her daughter asked, ''Haven't I been a *pretty* good girl today?'' ''That question,'' said the mother, ''went through me like a knife. I had been quick enough to correct her when she did wrong, but when she had tried to behave,

I had not noticed it. I had put her to bed without one word of appreciation.''

Focusing on Success

The best motivators know that one reason to recognize achievement is to help people concentrate on images of themselves succeeding, and that such mental exercises have an undeniable effect on performance.

Arthur Gordon told of hunting on a mild December afternoon in the Georgia low country:

A single-barreled, 20-gauge shotgun, given to me for Christmas, had made me the proudest 13-year-old in Georgia. On my first hunt, moreover, by a lucky freak, I had managed to hit the only bird I got a shot at. My heart almost burst with excitement and pride.

The second hunt was a different story. My companion was an elderly judge, a friend of my father's. He looked rather like a bloodhound, with a seamed brown face and hooded eyes and had the easy tolerance that comes from knowing the worst about the human race but liking people just the same. I had some misgivings about hunting with the Judge because I stood in awe of him, and wanted mightily to please him. And I walked straight into humiliation.

We found plenty of birds, and the Judge knocked down one or two on every covey rise. I, on the other hand, didn't touch a feather. I tried everything: shooting over, under, soon, late. Nothing made any difference. And the more I missed, the tenser I got.

Then old Doc, the pointer, spotted a quail in a clump of palmetto. He froze, his long tail rigid. Something in me froze, too, because I knew I was facing one more disgrace.

This time, however, instead of motioning me forward, the Judge placed his gun carefully on the ground. "Let's set a minute," he suggested . . . . Then, slowly, he said, "Your dad was telling me you hit the first quail you shot at the other day. That right?"

"Yes, sir," I said miserably. "Just luck, I guess."

"Maybe," said the Judge. "But that doesn't matter. Do you remember exactly how it happened? Can you close your eyes and see it all in your mind?"

I nodded, because it was true. I could summon up every detail: the bird exploding from under my feet, the gun seeming to point itself, the surge of elation, the warmth of the praise. . . .

"Well, now," the Judge said easily, "you just sit here and relive that shot a couple of times. Then go over there and kick up that bird. Don't think about me or the dog or anything else. Just think about that one good shot you made the other day—and sort of keep out of your own way."

When I did what he said, it was as if a completely new set of reflexes had come into play. Out flashed the quail. Up went the gun, smoothly and surely, as if it had life and purpose of its own. Seconds later, Doc was at my knee, offering the bird.

I was all for pressing on, but the Judge unloaded his gun. "That's all for today, son," he said. "You've been focusing on failure all afternoon. I want to leave you looking at the image of success."

"There," said Gordon, "complete in two sentences, was the best advice I'd ever had, or ever would have."

What the Judge did for Gordon is similar to what we often try to do for our patients in psychotherapy. They come to our offices, wounded from some recent failure, with their self-esteem at a low ebb. They feel as if they can do nothing right, and indeed with such a negative self-concept, they tend to fulfill the self-prophecies. So to reverse that trend, we ask them to reach back and relive some successes. If they are quite depressed it sometimes takes some prodding for them to picture any time when they functioned well. But as they begin to talk and replay the mental tapes of themselves at their best, it is surprising how they are visibly picked up. They have often become so obsessed with recent failures that they have forgotten the good years.

Can We Give Too Much Self-Confidence?

Mr. Dave Grant, who teaches courses on maximum performance to many supervisors in business, says that managers often come up after the seminar and say, "You know, we don't want to make our employees feel *too* good about themselves, or they'll think they should have more pay or a bigger job. Sometimes they need to be taken down a peg or two, and it doesn't hurt to arrange for them to fail once in a while."

It is a pathetic way to run an organization—as if employees were like infants in danger of being spoiled. The best leaders take the opposite approach. They do everything possible to help their people succeed and gain more confidence in what they are doing. W. Somerset Maugham said, "The common idea that success spoils people by making them vain, egotistic and self-complacent is erroneous; on the contrary, it makes them for the most part humble, tolerant, and firm. Failure makes people bitter and cruel."

Our task, then, is to help people parlay their small accomplishments into even larger ones. And one way to assist that is to follow rule number seven: recognize and applaud achievement.

"Some are kissing mothers and some are scolding mothers, but it is love just the same, and most mothers kiss and scold together."
—PEARL S. BUCK

CHAPTER NINE

When to Praise and When to Reprimand

Some positive thinkers have the idea that the only way to get people to produce is with positive reinforcement. But using praise is only one of many ways to motivate. We are complicated people and we are nudged along by a host of complicated stimuli.

At a seminar once I heard a motivational speaker say that there are only two ways to motivate people: either with love or fear. And the only effective one, he claimed, is love. All of which is a lot of reductionist nonsense. In the first place, we are motivated by many more things than love and fear, and, in the second place, fear is one rather effective way to bring out the best in people. Every day of our lives we do things because we are motivated by fear. We avoid certain kinds of behavior at work to keep from losing our jobs. We drive at certain speeds because we fear the repercussions of doing otherwise. It is folly even to hope for a world where we are not motivated by fear, and it is permissive foolishness to try to create a family where we do not use some punishment, or an office where we do not reprimand employees. We ought to employ the carrot more than the stick, but the stick has its uses.

Rule number eight, then, for bringing out the best in people is:

EMPLOY A MIXTURE OF POSITIVE AND NEGATIVE REINFORCEMENT

When John Wooden arrived at UCLA the basketball team had just ended a 12-13 losing season. He immediately set about building what became the most spectacular record in the collegiate history of the sport. When Wooden retired in 1975 he had coached the UCLA basketball team to 10 national championships in 12 years, a record unapproached by any other coach. He was called "The Wizard of Westwood" because he could win with tall men and short men. One year his was the smallest team compared to the competition ever to win a national championship.

Two research psychologists, Roland G. Tharp and Ronald Gallimore, studied Wooden's coaching methods in some detail during his 1974-75 season. After watching 15 practice sessions to see how he talked to his players on the floor, they found that in contrast to the techniques advocated by many behavior modifiers, praise was a minor feature of Wooden's teaching methods. Total positive social reinforcements, verbal and nonverbal, constituted only 7% of his total action. Negative statements added up to 14.6%. Wooden scolded twice as much as he rewarded.

But the precision of Wooden's negative statements is important to note. The researchers called it "scold/

instruction." That is, he would very often say, "Don't do it that way, do it *this* way," while he demonstrated the proper method. Wooden was never punitive or mean; he never used physical punishment, such as lap-running, but at times his reproofs could be withering: "I've been telling some of you for three years not to wind up when you throw the ball! Pass from the chest!"

Wooden's example can furnish us with several very specific suggestions about the use of negative reinforcement:

1. *Be certain that you're teaching them to avoid certain behavior, not to avoid you.* Wooden always kept a warm, trusting relationship with his players and often told them that next to his own flesh and blood they were the closest to him. This made it possible for him to get away with so many corrections and scoldings on the playing floor.

If our people go about their work constantly afraid of our wrath, they will not produce well. We will want our children, for instance, to *fear the consequences* of certain actions rather than fearing us. In an orderly and objective way we can point out to a child that life is a series of choices and that certain choices bring about certain results. Unsatisfactory grades cause them to lose privileges, and certain behavior gets them restricted. It is an essential lesson for them to learn as early as possible: if you touch the hot burner you get hurt, and if you turn in a poor report you get the repercussions.

This approach is vastly different from that of the tyrant. Certain leaders are unpredictable hotheads. If you happen to get on their wrong side, you are in trouble. They are vengeful and will do whatever is necessary to get back at you if you disappoint them. On the other hand, good motivators may be tough, but they are always fair, and they have your good and the good of the organization always before them. They do not waste time on vendettas.

2. *Follow the undesired behavior with immediate correction.* If there is any single fault with traditional punishing it is that the punishment often follows the behavior by such a long period that it is ineffective in changing the behavior. In fact some researchers want to distinguish between punishment, which comes after the event (in the case of the law, sometimes years after the event), and negative reinforcement, which comes immediately. Most studies indicate that when we punish people we only suppress the behavior. And it is effective only when we're there to threaten more punishment. When we're gone and there's no danger of getting caught, the behavior returns.

Contrast that with Wooden's technique. He scolded often, but he did it promptly enough that the behavior could change on the spot. And repetitiously using his scold/reinstruction method, the behavior pattern changed. He was out to shape habits.

3. *Establish a way to halt the negative stimulus as soon as the behavior stops.* Let's say that your child brings home a bad report card. You respond by withdrawing television for a month. A month is a long time and it is even longer until the next report card arrives, so the punishment is not very motivating now. And what happens if a worse report comes next time? Usually we don't say "Hmm, punishment isn't working,

let's try something else.'' Instead, we escalate the punishment, and this time we ground them longer. If threatening the employee doesn't work, dock their pay. If that doesn't work, suspend them. It becomes a vicious cycle and increasingly ineffective. As Victor Cline, in his book *How to Make Your Child a Winner*, says, ''Taking the bike or car away for 30 days instead of three is not 10 times more effective. In fact, it's usually counterproductive or even less effective. Why? The three-day loss of the bike or car makes your point very powerfully. But it means that in three days you can use the vehicle again as an effective deterrent or lever.''

If negative reinforcement is necessary, by all means offer a plan for the person to improve the situation. Claire, for instance, was a bright 16-year-old who was about to be expelled for truancy, poor grades, and fighting with her mother. She was threatening to run away, and her mother had taken away all money, the use of the telephone, and dating privileges as punishment. But the situation was only getting worse. Here's the plan that was worked out with the mother and daughter: one note from school each day, saying that she attended all classes, earned Claire telephone privileges for the day; four notes during the week earned one weekend date; and five earned two dates.

The mother was very doubtful at first, but the plan worked beyond belief. The lesson was this: when Claire was punished by loss of privileges, she showed no change until a definite way of earning the privileges back was offered.

4. One last suggestion. *If negative stimulus control doesn't seem to be working, try shaping the absence*

of the behavior. That is, give positive reinforcement to anything other than the undesired behavior. Karen Pryor, in her book *Don't Shoot the Dog*, tells how she used this method to modify her mother's behavior on the telephone. Her mother had been in her youth a fascinating, witty woman. But when she became an invalid living in a nursing home, the telephone conversations were usually, and sometimes exclusively, concerned with her problems—pain, loneliness, lack of money. Her complaints would turn to tears, and tears to accusations. The exchanges became so unpleasant that Pryor tended to duck the phone calls.

Pryor decided that there might be a better way. She began concentrating on her own behavior during the calls, deliberately extinguishing the complaints and tears by saying "Ah," and "Hmm," and "Well, well," when her mother complained, but not hanging up. Then she reinforced anything that was not a complaint—queries about the children, news from the nursing home, discussions of the weather, books, friends. These she responded to with enthusiasm.

To Pryor's astonishment, after 20 years of conflict, the proportion of tears and distress to laughter and chatting reversed within two months. The youthful, witty, interested mother returned.

Is such shaping manipulative? No more than John Wooden's coaching of his players and no more than the day-by-day methods we all use to influence the behavior of those around us. For all our talk about the merits of "love" versus "punishment," says James Q. Wilson, people are changed by routine interactions in which we convey "by word, tone, gesture, and expression, our approval or disapproval of the behavior of others."

Is Guilt a Legitimate Tool for the Motivator?

We turn now to one of the most difficult areas in which to find the proper balance when deciding which tools to use for motivation—the question of guilt. Two extreme views exist on this matter: (1) the position that guilt is never valid, that one should never be pushed by such a negative force into doing anything; and (2) the position that guilt is the most effective way of extracting conformity, especially from children.

Let's examine position number one first. This view is illustrated in its extreme by those who advocate that we avoid all ''shoulds.'' Pop psychologists are forever saying that people are to operate on ''I cans'' rather than ''I shoulds.'' They decry the admonition, ''You should call your mother.''

It is an ideal with a certain enticing sound to it— that we could live without ever using negative emotions to motivate anyone. But in reality, there is value in living by certain ''shoulds,'' and guilt is in fact a very valid emotion. When we do wrong, we ought to feel guilty. Prompted by that guilt, we can correct the wrong and avoid making the same mistake in the future.

But it is all too easy for the leader to use guilt excessively. In the short run it is both easy and effective, so parents often take the lazy way and regulate their children by this method. For an illustration of the devastating effect of such behavior, I turn to a patient recently in my office. Here is a woman now in her 50s, depressed and lethargic. In fishing to find the reasons she is so unhappy, I discover that she still runs scared because of the manipulative way her mother controlled her when she was a little girl. Here's the way it worked: if she did something to displease her mother, such as sneak off to a movie (it was a rigid home, in which many, many things were prohibited), her mother would never get angry; she simply got "hurt," and would pout for days. I asked my patient if she did such rebellious things often. "Oh, no," she replied, "I couldn't stand the way I felt when I knew I had hurt her." That mother used tears in a cruel way. By pouting and crying she kept the child's emotions on a string like a puppet, and the residual guilt lingers 40 years later.

It is important to distinguish between neurotic guilt and legitimate guilt, as Paul Tournier does in his splendid book, *Guilt and Grace*. Legitimate guilt is that which stems from knowledge that we have erred and which leads to correcting our course. Neurotic guilt is that which lingers long after any corrective measures have been taken, and is crippling rather than constructive. We need not walk on eggshells with our children for fear of leaving them with lingering guilt, and we should not hide our emotions when our kids disappoint us. The crucial difference in the manipulative parent is that he or she conjures up tears and anger in order to control the child.

So the question to ask yourself is this: Am I pouting or am I angry just to teach a child (or an employee) a lesson, or is this my genuine emotion? The relationship becomes neurotic and manipulative when we teach our children that mom's or dad's feelings are the most important reason for action. Instead our aim should be to teach them that there are certain laws of right and wrong in the universe and that they ought to make choices carefully, considering the results. And we will try to avoid the lament, "How could you do such a thing and hurt your mother so?"

Tom Edwards, who in addition to being an excellent writer is also a master teacher of junior high students, makes the distinction this way: "Our aim is not to control people, but rather to point out consequences and give choices to people. That way it is not manipulation but motivation."

The proper way to use negative tools for motivation is not an easy question for any of us who are dealing with people. What is the proper balance between negative and positive reinforcement? For now, let us agree that praising should far outweigh scolding, and that in the long run what we are aiming for in our use of fear and guilt is an allegiance to high values rather than fear of our displeasure.

"People are failures, not because they are stupid, but because they are not sufficiently impassioned."
—BURT STRUTHERS

CHAPTER TEN

The Will to Win

For most millionaires, the amassing of money eventually becomes a game. They no longer work because they need the income, but because they love competition. They enjoy pitting their skills against the business world.

This instinct to compete appears to be inborn in most of us; otherwise the world would not enjoy games. And therein lies a very strong—as well as very dangerous—basis for motivating people. Sales organizations use the technique constantly, with contests that hold out a new car or a vacation trip or a prestige award at the yearly banquet. If one wants to motivate an elementary school to raise money for a new computer, the best way is to run a contest among the classes and keep the race as close as possible. If the daily totals are prominently displayed so that every teacher and student can see their standing (and know that everyone else is looking at them too), the enthusiasm can be built to a feverish pitch. The amount of the prize is not nearly so important as the thrill of competing.

Charles Schwab, who supervised all of Andrew Carnegie's steel mills, had a mill manager whose men were not producing their quota of work. ''I've coaxed the men; I've pushed them; I've threatened them with damnation and being fired," the manager told Schwab. "But nothing works. They just won't produce."

It was the end of the day, just as the day shift was leaving and the night shift was coming on. "Give me a piece of chalk," Schwab said. Then, turning to the nearest man he asked, "How many heats did your shift make today?"

"Six."

Without another word, Schwab chalked a big figure 6 on the floor and walked away.

When the night shift came in, they saw the 6 and asked what it meant. "The big boss was in here today," the day men said, "and he chalked on the floor the number of heats we made."

The next morning Schwab walked through the mill again. The night shift had rubbed out 6, and replaced it with a big 7. When the day shift reported for work the next morning they saw the big 7 chalked on the floor. So the night shift thought they were better than the day shift, did they? Well, they would show them a thing or two. The men pitched in with enthusiasm and when they quit that night, they left behind them an enormous, swaggering 10. Things were stepping up.

Shortly, this mill, which had been lagging way behind in production, was turning out more work than any other mill in the industry. And what was the principle? Here is Schwab's description of it: "The way to get things done is to stimulate competition. I do not mean in a sordid, money-getting way, but in the desire to excel."

The idealists will try to tell us that when we get people to compete against each other we are using a form of manipulation and that the aggressive instinct should be discouraged rather than encouraged. As we shall see later, anger-fueled aggression can indeed be dangerous, but the fact of the matter is that we are all competitive by nature, and such an impulse can help people achieve things they would never accomplish otherwise. Athletics provide a good example. Every runner, every swimmer, every football player knows that he or she performs best when pitted against others. It is the comparison, the desire to excel and to win, that pushes them on. School rivalries, neck-and-neck competition with another company, lists of the 10 best employees—these are all powerful stimulants.

So rule number nine for bringing out the best in people is this:

APPEAL SPARINGLY TO THE COMPETITIVE URGE

I say sparingly because competition has only limited usefulness. If factory workers are pitted against each other excessively, they will feel manipulated and they will resent it. Moreover, if too much aggression is unleashed among employees or students, they begin to stab each other in the back. At highly competitive schools, students will even steal essential books from the reserve shelf to prevent others from succeeding. These excesses, however, do not disprove the value of healthy competition, and they should not deter us from using comparisons to stimulate strong effort.

A Nobel Laureate on Competition

An ideal balance of cooperation and competition is to be found in the work of Arno A. Penzias, who in 1978 shared the Nobel Prize in physics for his discoveries of what has become known as cosmic blackbody radiation. He is now vice-president for research at Bell Laboratories. Penzias's family had barely escaped the Nazi persecution of the Jews, and when they landed in New York the first week of January 1940, it was a foreign, alien world. His father eventually became a superintendent in various apartment buildings in the Bronx, collecting garbage out of the dumbwaiters and stoking the furnaces. His mother went to work in the garment district.

"I suppose everybody is unhappy in junior high school," Penzias says. "I had a foreign accent. I never really learned kids' ways. By the time I could speak English well, I could not play the games well." He had a hard time in high school physics, but was able to go on to the City College of New York, partly because "the price was right," he says, meaning that it was tuition-free. M.I.T. turned him down for graduate school, and he enrolled at Columbia, where he barely survived.

They let just about anybody in . . . . People came in with degrees in English. Then they failed half the class. They just flunked people out like mad. It never seemed to occur to anyone that they were ruining people's lives. It seemed to me to be a sort of mechanical, mindless grinding of human beings. . . .

I will never forget my first exam. Townes gave it, in an optics course. It was an open-book exam with five questions. I couldn't do any of them. By the time I got to number five, I was in a cold sweat. I was sitting in this room, and I had just gone through the first four questions. None of them could I answer—not any one. I got to number five, and I looked around and saw that everybody else was working. I asked myself, "What are the odds that I am the dumbest person in this room?" . . . I got a fifty-four, which, it turned out, was the second-highest mark in the class. Townes, as it happened, was just beginning to think about lasers. So he had wanted to learn about optics, and on the exam he asked about things that *he* was interested in.

Penzias claims that he graduated by the skin of his teeth: "There were two things that I was good at. One was that I had an ability to organize things in mechanical terms, to build things—and the other was that I had, and have, a great ability to endure pain. These were the two things that got me through Columbia."

Would Penzias have been able to go on to win the Nobel Prize without first learning to endure pain in such a competitive environment as Columbia? It is hard to say, of course, but now that he directs research, he certainly has not eliminated competition. "Nobody gives me a quota that tells me I have to turn out so many patents," he says. "But there is pressure all over—pressure from the Japanese, who are competing with us, and pressure from within to help the light-wave people, help terminal people, help the switching people, help every single group as fast as we can. I demand a certain standard of myself and of everybody else." Competition is always a factor for highly motivated people. The trick is to know how to use it in balance.

When Comparison Backfires

There is a fine line between using comparisons to criticize and using them to inspire. Comparison is ill-used when a wife says to her husband, "If Jack down the street works hard all day and isn't too tired to paint his house, why can't you?'' Many of us have had that technique tried on us for years. Our parents said, ''Why can't you bring home good grades like your sister?'' Those are negative messages which debilitate us rather than empower us. Comparison well used says, ''You know, Tom, when I see what the neighbors have done with their yard, it makes me want to get out and do something terrific with ours too. What do you think?'' The simple listing of how people in an office gave to the United Way, for instance, can be a powerful tool for getting people to give more. They want to look good before their friends. Keeping in mind that the goal is not to shame them but inspire them, we can impart the healthy message: if others can do it, so can we. It is an old principle of fund raising that ''financial influence flows downhill.'' In other words, a good money-raising campaign solicits the biggest contributors first, then asks them to call on their friends. The friends may be capable of giving less, yet they will dig down into their pockets far better when called on by this person whom they know to be a generous giver. It is the old healthy competitive instinct. We do much less than we are capable of until someone shows us greater possibilities.

Anger as Motivator

We now turn to an emotion which is allied to competition, but which is a further extension of that passion: anger. Here again, the idealists might suppose that the only way to inspire people is to appeal to their benevolent instincts, but the best motivators usually appeal to the anger in people as well. Why? Because enormous energies reside deep within us and come to the surface when we get angry. Martin Luther said: "When I am angry I can write, pray, and preach well, for then my whole temperament is quickened, my understanding sharpened, and all mundane vexations and temptations gone." A little righteous indignation seems to bring out the best in the national personality. The United States was born when 56 patriots got angry enough to sign the Declaration of Independence. We put a man on the moon because Sputnik made us mad at being number two in space.

This motivational principle is well-illustrated by Lee Iacocca's use of *The Wall Street Journal*. In 1979 the paper had published a scorching editorial criticizing Chrysler's mismanagement and saying that the nearly bankrupt company should be allowed to "die with dignity."

Iacocca got lots of mileage out of that quote. Rather than allowing it to damage him, or ignoring it and hoping people would forget it, he turned it around and used it to arouse passionate sympathy for his company's cause. Here is an excerpt from one of his speeches:

> *The Wall Street Journal* advised me to let Chrysler Corporation "die with dignity." After all we were flat broke. Our plants were industrial museums. The Michigan State Fairgrounds were full of our unsold cars.
>
> I got mad. . . . My colleagues in Highland Park got mad. Tens of thousands of Chrysler people all across America got mad. Our labor unions, our suppliers, and our lenders all got mad. We got so mad, we banded together, we talked things over, and working together, we fixed what was wrong at Chrysler.
>
> We doubled our productivity. We rejuvenated our factories. We cut our costs. We started building the

highest quality cars and trucks made in America. In short, we turned things around. Now, we're selling cars and making lots of money. . . . This story has a moral. Wonderful things can happen when Americans get mad. I think some well-directed anger can cure most of what's wrong in America today.

Very few people listening to Iacocca's speech could keep from having some visceral reaction, for such a speech makes you want to support the underdog.

When Anger Is Legitimate

Is anger seen as a negative force in the Bible? The Hebrew words that are translated "anger" or "angry" in the Old Testament occur almost 455 times, and nearly 375 of these refer to God's anger. Christ blazed with anger at the scribes and Pharisees, and the Scriptures paint life in general as warfare: we wrestle against forces of evil, against principalities and powers of darkness.

Any powerful motivational speaker uses the entire panoply of emotions to stir the listener, and anger is certainly one of them. Mark Twain was fond of saying that to hold a crowd you must alternate between wooing them and abusing them, and all good platform speakers, like good coaches, will occasionally display anger at their audiences. Moreover, they will be seen arousing anger in their people as Iacocca did in his famous speech about *The Wall Street Journal*.

The Advantages of Having a Common Enemy

Appealing to anger and the competitive spirit does another thing: it tends to pull people together. A large family may have lots of sibling squabbles at the dinner table, but if a child is criticized by someone from the outside and that fact is aired at the table, cohesiveness builds in a hurry. And a congregation that is fighting internally can quickly forget its intramural differences if it is inspired to take on some common enemy.

In fact, churches furnish us with interesting microcosms for watching how group morale is built and destroyed. For all our religious talk about love, I have never seen a congregation genuinely fired up which did not have the conviction that they were fighting some common enemy. The adversaries may be very different for different types of churches, but it seems essential to find something to oppose.

Unscrupulous Appeals to Our Anger

We must not overlook the fact that propagandists can fan the flame of hatred to horrible ends, and that wars and lynchings are also the result of group anger. Hitler aroused enormous energy and cohesiveness by using the Jews as scapegoats, and when Jim Jones convinced 912 people to commit suicide together, he did it by constructing a paranoid, illusionary world for his followers to hate. Both are illustrations of appeals to anger which have run amuck.

To avoid such perversions, we must appeal sparingly to people's competitive instincts and we must choose our enemies carefully. There is nothing wrong with hate, so long as it is directed at the right objects: cruelty, selfishness, deceit, manipulation, infliction of pain on helpless victims. Nor is there anything wrong with rallying a group to work harder because they are angry, so long as we give them legitimate objects for their anger and refrain from creating straw men in order to pull people to our side. Our world contains plenty of injustices, plenty of wrongs to be righted, and plenty of abusive people to oppose without having to create any artificial receptacles for our hatred.

"What we call society is really a vast network of mutual agreements."
—S. I. HAYAKAWA

"It is amazing how much people can get done if they do not worry about who gets the credit."
—SANDRA SWINNEY

CHAPTER ELEVEN

How to Get People to Cooperate with Each Other

We must now discuss the elusive topic of group morale. What is it about some leaders that enables them to so construct their group or their family that there is always high *esprit de corps* and a tight allegiance to one another? And why is it that others who seem to be inspiring enough in one-to-one exchanges always end up with groups that fracture and fight and can never get anything done efficiently?

The leader who can learn the laws of group morale becomes a highly valuable commodity, for not only does good *esprit de corps* enable people to get the job done in half the time, it also draws in new people. Some of the most successful churches, for instance, are led by pastors who do not have magnetic personalities. Their success is due rather to the skill with which they build an enthusiastic, cohesive congregation. So in such cases people are drawn not so much to the leader but to the group feeling—the high-energy atmosphere. Good leaders set out to do far more than build allegiance to themselves, which is important, of course, but it is not enough. It is also necessary to build into the organization an allegiance to each other.

Rule number ten for bringing out the best in people is:

*P*LACE A PREMIUM ON COLLABORATION

Organizers of successful groups base their work on a fundamental fact about the makeup of the human personality: most of us can function best when teamed up with at least one other person. I think, for instance, of the encouragement and solidarity that exists between many husbands and wives who are building something together. Writing is the hardest work I've ever attempted, and I quite literally could not do it without Diane. This chapter is being written at St. Andrew's Priory, a Benedictine retreat 80 miles away from my home in Los Angeles. A few days of solitude like this are a wonderful stimulant, but I would not be typing here at midnight if I did not feel very closely linked to the woman asleep alone in our bed tonight. She's there not because she likes solitude but because she knows that it is terribly important for me to get this chapter finished and in the mail this week. In the discouraging years when all my work was rejected by publishers, I simply would have quit had it not been for the cheerful, blithe confidence Diane continued to display. One person against the many is seldom a match. But two people! That is a different story. If you can find one other person who will join you in your quest, you have not doubled your capabilities, you have increased them exponentially.

The same principle applies to losing weight, abstaining from alcohol, or learning a language—there is power in numbers. Being in a group hardens your resolve, and gives you momentum for bursting through obstacles.

The Need to Belong

In every person there resides a basic need that in the technical books on this topic is called "the affiliative motive." Each of us likes to belong to some group of tightly-knit people where we are known and accepted, where we are committed to each other, and where we know that the other members of the group will be loyal to us if we are in trouble. It is the old tribal instinct. Ideally, this will occur in our families, where people forgive anything. When such devotion is cultivated in families, people may stray away for a while, but they inevitably return. If such a loyalty develops in a group of employees it has a similar adhesive effect. People will stay on your staff even when they could earn more at another company, for an important psychological need is being met by their employer—the need to belong. It is not, as some suppose, that anyone has much allegiance to a company. The "company man" is a phenomenon of the past, if in fact such a person ever existed. Who has ever had much loyalty to a company? But we do have lots of ties to the rather amorphous entity comprised of people with whom we have worked, to the traditions we have established for quality, and to the younger people who have come into the company and whose futures depend on what we build together.

The following pages detail some characteristics that high-morale organizations seem to have in common.

Quality Control

The best groups always take a great deal of responsibility for their own standards. Poor leaders make the mistake of remaining the sole custodian of quality control, whereas good leaders encourage people to hold each other accountable for excellence.

Here is an example from manufacturing. A friend bought a foundry a few years ago. "Among the employees," he said, "I found a group of old-timers who were a clique and stayed to themselves, but they consistently turned out the best work in the shop. When they got together to drink coffee, they would show each other their work, scoff at something that was poorly done, and admire what was good.

"I wasn't about to tamper with that clique and move the men around, because not only did each one of them take pride in his work, there was also a strange group pride at work there—it was important that they not allow anyone among them to fail. The consequence was that they all did better work because of the inner competition and loyalty." That foundry owner had learned the important lesson of allowing group morale to do much of his work for him.

Here is an example of the same principle at work in a family. At a banquet recently I sat next to a charming woman whose six children had attended schools like Harvard, Stanford, and Wellesley. They were all achievers, with not a bad apple among them. "How in the world did you inspire them?" I asked.

"Everyone asks me that," she laughed, "and the embarrassing thing is that I don't think I did much. For instance, I never told them to do their homework or scolded them when they brought home poor grades. They seemed to motivate one another. For instance, I remember the day one of our daughters brought home a report card that was less than it should have been. I didn't say anything and put it back on the kitchen counter. But when her older brother came home, he looked at it, snorted, then went to her room and gave her a big pep talk. I'm not sure exactly what he said, but among other things he convinced her that there were family standards which she was supposed to maintain, and that if she didn't do well it would be a reflection on everyone. It must have been some speech, because she dramatically raised her grades on the next report card. She looked up to her brother and loved him so much, she would have done anything to stay in his good graces."

That mother had wisely done almost exactly what the good executive does: she had built a group-wide appreciation for excellence, then let the group maintain it.

All for One and One for All

A second characteristic of high-morale groups is this: everyone believes that the leaders are putting the group's welfare first. There is always a large question in a person's mind when deciding how enthusiastically to join in any organization: Are these leaders out for themselves and merely trying to whip up enthusiasm for their projects, or will they make sure that this enterprise is beneficial for all of us?

In companies where the prevailing philosophy is to get as much from the employees as possible and to give them as little as possible, new workers catch on very quickly and have no compunctions about sabotaging the management and carrying home supplies in their pockets every evening. By contrast, consider Andrew Carnegie, who took the position that "no man can become rich without himself enriching others," and built a high-morale organization that indeed made him rich. If we can convince a group of people that it is all for one and one for all, great power can be released.

Jean Riboud, head of the multinational Schlumberger company, says that the best way to get on in the world is to "make people believe it is to their advantage to help you." Such a policy can be highly manipulative if we try to convince people that it is to their advantage to help us when it is *not*. On the other hand, if we believe in a project and are committed to collaboration as a means of achieving it, and if we intend to share the dividends with our people, then we should be saying it to them over and over.

The same principle applies to family leadership. When children believe that family rules are only for the convenience of the parents, it is not very motivating. A girl may be convinced that her mother insists on certain kinds of behavior only because she does not want to be embarrassed before her friends. But if children can be persuaded that the family exists for everyone's benefit and that the rules have been set to help members function best, they will be much more sympathetic to those rules. Strong leadership—even autocratic leadership—can be tolerated by most people so long as it is clear that the leader is devoted to the good of all.

In his book *American Caesar,* William Manchester tries to analyze the remarkable loyalty which Colonel Douglas MacArthur elicited from his men during World War I. When it was all over, MacArthur won seven Silver Stars, two Distinguished Service Crosses, and the Distinguished Service Medal. Those medals were in part due to his bravery, of course, but they were also due to his ability to elicit a fierce loyalty from his troops. And how did he do that? Here is William Manchester's list: "He was closer to their age than other senior officers, he shared their discomforts and their danger, and he adored them in return." That last phrase is the key—"He adored them in return." For all his egomania and emotional distortions, MacArthur had one redeeming virtue which fired his men's passions: he cared for them deeply. Highly motivated groups know that their leader loves them profoundly and will be loyal to them to the end.

Promises

The Center for Creative Leadership in Greensboro, North Carolina, recently studied 21 derailed executives—successful people who were expected to go higher in the organization but who reached a plateau in their careers and were fired or were forced to retire early. They were compared with 20 "arrivers"—those who made it all the way to the top.

The researchers found the two groups astonishingly alike. Every one of the 41 executives possessed remarkable strengths, and every one was flawed by one or more significant weaknesses. So a person can make a lot of mistakes and have certain weaknesses, evidently, and still rise to success. But closer study of the derailed executives showed that certain types of flaws kept cropping up in a large number of them, and that one error, when committed, always led to their downfall. The researchers called it "the unforgivable sin—betraying a trust." Integrity here means more than simple honesty. It embodies consistency and predictability built over time that says, "I will do exactly what I say I will do when I say I will do it. If I change my mind, I will tell you well in advance so you will not be harmed by my actions."

Some of us make too many promises to too many people, and nothing demoralizes a group more quickly. Rene McPherson, who was chief executive officer of the Dana Corporation, when asked about the phenomenal success of that organization, says: "The way you treat an employee is closely observed by all other employees. They decide whether you and your company can be trusted on the basis of that data." One might suppose that in a large organization managers could get away with treating a few people ruthlessly, but just one such example can destroy a whole group's morale. As McPherson says, everyone is watching how you treat that employee with the assumption that they will be treated in the same way.

Families also keep an eye on their leadership for such tip-offs. If a father promises his son a car when he reaches 17 and then doesn't deliver, he not only has destroyed that boy's trust but has damaged the

family's spirit as well, for all the other family members
have been watching that betrayal. It behooves us to go
to considerable lengths to show people that we will
make good on our contracts to them; otherwise they
will keep brakes on their enthusiasm.

Fairness

Another demoralizing tactic is to distribute rewards
unfairly. Much research has been done on what
is labeled *equity theory*, but which is instinctively
known by every good leader: people's motivation col-
lapses completely if they feel someone else is being
compensated or rewarded differently.

A fascinating study was done in 1972 by Schmitt
and Marwel in which pairs of workers were given the
choice of working separately for a little money, or
working with another person for more money. The
catch was this: although both would be paid more, if
they worked together one was to be paid more than
the other for the same job. It was an unequal distri-
bution of compensation, with no apparent reasons for
the unfairness. *Fully 40% of the pairs chose to work
for less money than to accept the lopsided compensation.* The study dramatizes our powerful need to be
treated fairly.

It is probably the reason so-called merit pay for
teachers is not the answer to America's educational
failings. You do not motivate people by coming in to
a school and labeling 15% of staff as "master teachers." It may motivate them, but what happens to the
other 85% who were not so designated? Think of your
own job. Suppose someone came into your place of
work, evaluated everybody's performance, labeled

15% of those doing the same work as "master workers," and gave them a 25% wage premium over everybody else. Would productivity go up or down? To ask the question is to answer it.

Lester C. Thurow tells about teaching in two different university economics departments. Both were famous for their research, but one was famous for its good teaching while the other was infamous for its bad teaching. There were no significant differences in the ways in which people were paid or in the size of the salary differentials. "Good teaching," he decided, "occurred in one because there was a strong social ethos that good teaching was your first responsibility and would be rewarded with peer respect." That whole ethos could have been destroyed if the teachers were treated unequally.

"Nice guys" often make poor bosses for a similar reason. If you bend the rules for certain people, it causes confusion among the staff and a drop in morale. By trying to stay on good terms with everyone and making too many exceptions to company rules, you appear to care more for the happiness of particular individuals than the well-being of the whole working group. It violates one of motivation's basic principles—fairness.

The Preservation of the Individual

Another ingredient for good morale is closely allied to the one we've just been discussing: the members must know that they will never get lost in the group. Here is a paradox. We can allow ourselves to be absorbed into a group most readily when we are assured that the leaders will value our individuality.

Collectivism scares us if we think that people will become expendable for the sake of the larger group.

When A. W. Clausen was head of the Bank of America he was asked by *The Harvard Business Review* about his rise from clerk to chief executive officer. In that revealing interview, Clausen talked with genuine affection about various colleagues in his firm, about the older executives from whom he had learned the ropes, and about the lower echelon employees. It was obvious that people were important to him.

An illustration of how this policy works followed the interview. It was the story of a middle-aged Bank of America executive who had a great deal of pride. He had been with the firm for 25 years when his performance deteriorated. The spark wasn't there anymore, and he was absent for long periods of time for medical reasons. His supervisors decided that he was underchallenged, so they moved him to a different assignment at a very busy branch. After 30 days, the old habits returned. He couldn't remember customers he'd worked with just a day before, and he'd go home early with chest pains.

The district manager asked him if he thought any portion of his illness could be psychosomatic. "Yes, I do," he said. "The pains are severe, believe me, but when I'm tested, the doctors don't find anything." His superiors then offered him a lower-level job with less pressure and responsibility, but where he would lose his title. "I couldn't handle that," he said, and his boss replied, "I don't blame you. I don't think I could either."

Many companies would have given up at this point and terminated the man. But for Bank of America it was back to the drawing board. Further investigation showed that the only time he was motivated occurred each evening when he worked as a volunteer in a charitable organization. His wife had his clothes laid out when he arrived home from work, and he hurried to his second office where he put in several hours of pleasurable work. To the credit of the bank, they looked at the volunteer job to determine what he found appealing there and eventually found a similar post in their company. At last count, he was, after two years in the new job, happy and productive. "It was quite an experience," said the district manager, "to watch someone so totally disenchanted with himself and his career meet this problem head on and walk through it. All of us walked through it. It was a great feeling, to tell you the truth."

Clausen's group knew that if you can salvage one such employee, it has repercussions far beyond that one person. Many other workers are watching to see if the individual person actually *does* count in your company.

Fun

The last characteristic of high-morale organizations is that they seem to have fun together. Too often the parent or the manager is guilty of growling, "OK, we've had enough fun, let's get back to work," when the best work could be done while having fun. Thomas A. Edison once received a letter from a solemn stockholder. "A vice-president of your company," he wrote, "doesn't have a proper sense of dignity of his position and of his association with you. I'm told sometimes his laugh can be heard through his door and all over the office."

Edison sent the letter to the vice-president, tied to the framed picture of a laughing, jolly friar. "Hang this picture in the entrance hall," he wrote. "Have everyone around the office look at it. Let it be a constant reminder that good business is never done except in a reasonably good-humored frame of mind and on a human basis."

I was interviewed once by a committee that laughed more frequently than any group of people I had ever seen. They had been meeting at least once a week for long sessions, and, though they were very different individuals, they worked together with a minimum of friction and with great enthusiasm. The secret, I think, was in their laughter. The chairman, Harry Griffin, had structured the group that way from its inception. His philosophy was: "We're going to be together for hundreds of hours before this job is done. If we choose, we can grit our teeth and try to get it over with as soon as possible, with no monkey business allowed. Or we can decide to have some fun every time we meet. I vote for having fun." That did not mean that they wasted time but that in their meetings they always laughed. There was lots of affectionate ribbing of one another, and the result was a wonderful *esprit de corps,* which in turn enabled them to finish their task months sooner than expected.

People never get to laugh as much as they'd like or have as much fun as they want, so if you can construct your class, your team, or your committee so that laughter breaks out frequently, you'll have people clamoring to join your group.

We were created to tease and play. Anne Sullivan was, as we've said, a stern taskmaster and a very firm disciplinarian with Helen Keller. How was she able to get away with that, given her high-spirited young student? In part it was because she mixed laughter and play with the rigors of their study and work together. Immediately after they had learned to communicate words with their fingers, Anne taught Helen how to play. "I had not laughed since I became deaf," Miss Keller says. "One day she came into the room laughing merrily. She put my hand on her bright, mobile face and spelled 'laugh.' Then she tickled me into a burst of mirth that gladdened the hearts of the family. Next she guided me through the motions of romping— swinging, tumbling, hopping, skipping—suiting the spelled word to each act. In a few days I was another child, pursuing new discoveries through the witchery of Teacher's finger-spelling."

Steps to Building *Esprit de Corps*

So far we have discussed certain qualities which characterize the best groups: quality control, mutual loyalty, integrity, fairness, the assurance that members will be valued as individuals, and play. Now let's turn to some specific techniques which a leader can use to enhance the team spirit we've been describing.

1. *Reward cooperation.* Some organizations are structured so that if you are a part of a working group that produces strong results, you may get nothing. If, on the other hand, you torpedo the success of others in order to chalk up personal achievements, you are praised. Obviously, such a policy invites backstabbing and bad morale. If it is only the prima donnas in the company who get the strokes, your organization will

respond by producing more prima donnas. If it is the team players who are rewarded, your organization will produce lots of collaborators.

2. *Assign responsibility for group morale to the group itself.* Peer pressure is always more successful than pressure from the top, so impress on the people in your committee or your family that part of their job is creating the right mood. That way everyone is accountable for the level of morale. In short, you have taught them to be motivators.

3. *Plan occasions when people can be away together.* A curious thing happens when you take a group of people away from their ordinary surroundings. They become more creative, more open to new ideas, and they form strong bonds with each other rather quickly. So good leaders often take a day or two with their group at some location where they can cement their relationships, undistracted by regular routines. I often speak at meetings of law or accounting partners at resort areas, where the firm has wisely retreated for a few days of regrouping, airing their objectives and problems, and getting better attuned to each other. When sales organizations want to weld their people into an enthusiastic group, they invite them to a hotel and a weekend of meetings. Comparing notes and joining in high-energy group sessions, they discover a camaraderie that did not exist in their casual contact with each other in the office. Because they are together without any opportunity to talk to other people and get pulled down by some pessimistic voice, all competition for their energies has been excluded.

4. *Assign a high value to communication.* More often than not, when a group is fractured and people

begin to fight each other, it is because of misunder-standings and small acts of inconsideration which have escalated into major grievances. In the next chapter, I will suggest some ways to eliminate intramural squabbling, but one way to head it off early is to make sure that there are regular opportunities for talk among the members. Families, for instance, need to do lots of communicating. It is a simple courtesy to leave notes on the kitchen counter telling the rest of the family where you've gone and when you expect to be back. Such habits are simple, but they do much to smooth the intercrossings which we must regularly make with one another.

Many of us hate business meetings and committee meetings, but as much as we dislike them and as little as they sometimes may seem to accomplish, it is very important to give people an opportunity to talk about their activities, ask questions, and test future plans on each other. There is nothing that makes us feel shut out of a group faster than to discover that other members have been informed about a topic when we have been left in the dark. Organizations fracture when information is dispensed primarily by the grapevine, for the grapevine is notoriously discriminatory—certain people will know and others will not, and the people who are left out are certain to be malcontents.

Management by Friendship

Management, like parenting, is at its best when it is collaboration. The cynical statement of this principle is, "It's not what you know, it's who you know." But *both* what you know and who you know are important. We do business with someone who proves to be knowledgeable, reliable, and enjoyable to work with, and we build a relationship of trust, where we exchange favors and swap information. Over the years it turns out to the mutual benefit of everyone. The famous Dallas businessman John Stemmons, when asked for business advice said this: "Find some people who are comers, who are going to be achievers in their own field, no matter what it is, and people you can trust. Then grow old together." Many people go all through life without discovering that principle. They assume that their success or failure in life is all their own doing, when in fact much of it is because others do or do not support them in their undertakings.

Group loyalty is not blind allegiance, and it is not harboring incompetence. Nor is it the sort of prejudicial blindness which supposes that everyone is wrong except our little group. Rather it is open-eyed acknowledgment that the people within our group may have their failings, but because we are a group and because we have a history of mutual allegiance, we support one another. That is our contract.

*"Be angry but do not sin; do not let the
sun go down on your anger."*
—St. Paul

CHAPTER TWELVE

---

*How to Deal
with the Abrasive
Troublemaker*

Some have contagiously enthusiastic personalities and know how to give good pep talks,
but they find themselves unable to cope when
confronted with an abrasive troublemaker in the group.
And unfortunately just one explosive individual can
ruin the chemistry of an organization and cause all its
enthusiasm to vanish before one's eyes.

Rule number eleven then, for bringing out the best
in people is:

---

*B*UILD INTO THE GROUP
AN ALLOWANCE FOR STORMS

For some, the only way to deal with troublemakers
is to replace them. But there is no way to get
away from troublesome personalities, and if we do not
learn to handle them, we will be running from difficult
situations all our lives. When Dr. David Cowie was a

young pastor, he was head of a church in Los Angeles that was growing rapidly and doing well, but on the governing board he had a man who was both a negative thinker and a very cantankerous critic. Finally the situation got so bad that he resigned and took a new pastorate in Kansas City. "But," he lamented, "the week I arrived at my new church I went to the board meeting to meet the leaders, and there, sitting at the conference table, was the same guy!"

Cowie was right. They may have different faces and different names, but no matter where we go, troublesome people are going to be waiting for us. It simply does not pay to flee from difficult interpersonal situations.

Robert Updegraff, writing many years ago about one's job, said:

A man should be grateful every hour of every day for the troubles of his job: they pay at least half his wage or salary. For if there were no troubles it would be easy to get someone to do his work for half, or even a third, of the pay he is getting. If he wants a bigger job, with a better income, he has to look for more troubles, and learn how to lick them. A bigger job will usually gravitate to him—often actually seek him out— if he is capable of coping with the problems and troubles that go with it. Especially is this true if he has cultivated the knack of doing everything pleasantly and with apparent ease and assurance. It is this special knack, which incidentally is perfectly possible for almost any man to cultivate, that usually puts the fancy edge on a salary.

Handling Rebellion

There is a problem for which every leader needs to be braced. It is the natural tendency of the follower to rebel against authority. Most people are a curious contradiction: they desire a dynamic leader to inspire them, and they will also be hostile toward the person who has any power over their destiny. So when every idea you propose is shot down and the group seems to resist every effort to build them up, it may be no more than the natural instinct to curb a leader's power. It is the rebellion that children feel against their parents, that students feel against their teachers, and that all employees will at one time or another feel toward their bosses. The higher we rise, the more we will be subject to this combination of admiration and anger.

One way, of course, to avoid any serious mutiny is to surround yourself with weak people and keep everything tightly within your control. But it is a hard way to live, and eventually, if the organization gets large enough, you will be forced to delegate. When you do that, a certain amount of conflict is certain to arise. Among other things, you will have people with talents that are more developed than yours, who know more about a given topic than you do, and to whom you must defer at times. The stronger these associates, the more certain they are to criticize you and to create sparks in your ranks. But such tension is not necessarily bad, and the best leaders are willing to invite these problems in order to have access to the strongest personnel. That is, they are not asking for carbon copies of themselves, but independent and creative thinkers who have minds of their own and who are strong enough to lead the people below them. The trouble with choosing yes-men to work under you is that they, in turn, will never be capable of leading others. Your aim is to grow leaders who can do your job for you, enabling you to rise to other things. In the process, you may have to put up with some testiness.

Defusion by Ventilation

Part of being a leader is that you must spend a considerable amount of energy absorbing other people's complaints. It is not the happiest way to spend one's time, but if a group is going to run smoothly people must have an opportunity to get the bile out of their systems. Providing this ventilation should not be an unbearable burden when you remind yourself that it is one of the ways you keep a group tightly motivated. What we are after is a positive-thinking cadre of people in which there is a minimum of backbiting, criticizing, and negative communication. The only way that will be possible is if the leader is willing to drain off a great deal of venom by getting potential troublemakers aside and hearing them out. Anger is inevitable, and it is much smarter to let it ventilate upward rather than to allow it to smolder down in the ranks, for it is such smoldering that often erupts into a major conflagration. In every organization, whether it is a family of four or a company of 100,000, the only way to keep a high level of enthusiasm is to build in adequate corridors for grievances.

Solving Conflict among Members of Your Group

At times, people's complaints will not be about your leadership but about others in their group. At the simplest level, this can be seen in a family where siblings fight and appeal to you to be the arbiter. The wise parent and the wise leader knows when to step in and when to allow the participants to work out their own problems. There is no rule of thumb, but if you are in charge you will at times become the referee. It is foolish to allow feuds to go on too long in any organization. Certain congregations never get anything accomplished because the pastor tries to please everyone and stays removed from differences of opinion. The boss who says, "I don't want to hear about the squabbles between you guys—this is for you to work out," is inviting trouble. At times you must go in, hear the sides, push the participants to a compromise, then throw all your weight behind the compromise. The good motivator tries not to lose anyone, but also never allows fighting to decimate the organization.

Dealing with the Perpetual Troublemaker

We must now talk about the difficulties all parents and all leaders have with the abrasive person who is always disruptive. Such persons exist in every group, and no one keeps a crowd motivated for a very long period without gaining some skill in dealing with the troublemaker. Here are some suggestions:

1. *Allow for some inexplicable behavior.* At management seminars and sales conventions, I am forever recommending that people build into their relationships some allowance for temporary insanity. The boundaries between neuroses and psychoses are much more vague than some clinicians would have us believe, and most supposedly normal people occasionally cross over the line of irrationality. So it helps to build into the contract a plan for storms.

2. *Try to ascertain the reason for the abrasiveness.* This is not always readily apparent. J. P. Morgan said, "A man always has two reasons for doing anything—a good reason and the real reason." There could be genuine grievances which can be heard and possibly rectified if you will do a little sleuth work.

3. *Determine just how disruptive the person is.* Again, this may not be readily apparent. Some people who have the reputation for being the group rebel are actually very much beloved by their peers. They may be regarded as good-natured complainers and are respected for their honesty, and in fact, the group may defend them vociferously if you try to dislodge them. You could realize too late that they were the outlet for many people's unspoken negative emotions.

4. *Ask for help.* "Never claim as a right what you can ask as a favor," advises John Churton Collins, and sometimes the most stubborn and uncooperative employees will melt when you ask for their advice or assistance. When you give impassioned pep talks they fear that you may be trying to manipulate them, but you can privately go to them and say, "Our group morale is in trouble and I haven't had much luck in improving it; you are obviously a person whom the group listens to, and I'm wondering if I can ask for some help from you." It may be the first time anyone has asked.

5. *Weigh the person's contribution.* If it turns out that the person *is* disruptive and destructive to morale, the next question should be: Just how valuable is this individual's contribution? Some mavericks will always be independent and hard to get along with, but they accomplish enough to outweigh the trouble they cause. This is especially true in fields where independent work

is at the heart of the organization's success. In some instances, it is performance—not conformance—that counts, and the rebellious star is worth hanging on to.

William James said that the essence of genius is to know what to overlook, and the president of a large university writes:

> It is my job to make it possible for the first-rate teacher to teach. Whether he gets along with his colleagues or with me—and very few of the really good teachers do either—is irrelevant. We certainly have a collection of problem children here, but boy, do they teach!

Such a policy will not work in every organization but it is a rule to apply whenever possible.

6. *If the problem is severe enough, remove the person.* This may sound as if it contradicts what I've just said about overlooking certain transgressions, but there is a vast difference between overlooking an irregularity because you choose to do so in the interests of creativity and, on the other hand, avoiding a problem because you don't like conflict. It is a weak leader who allows morale to be disrupted and the group's work torpedoed because he or she is afraid to punish, reprimand, and even dismiss. At times you must take a stand even if it means paring down the group.

7. *In all your dealings with troublemakers, appeal to the best side of the person.* In a fiery exchange, we unfortunately tend to assign permanence to emotions, when the best thing we could say would be, "Sam, I've known you a long time—long enough to know that this is not your best self speaking today, so I suggest we table all of this for now. We're both tired, so how about forgetting we had this conversation, and tomorrow morning we'll start over again?" Such an

assumption that this is not a malicious person, but simply a person having a bad day, can work wonders in some relationships. "Be gentle in your reprimands," St. Paul advised Timothy, and many relationships could be salvaged if that advice were heeded more generally. Most of us have seen business partnerships blow up and marriages collapse because someone spoke too soon. A good night's sleep or a weekend off would have been all that was required for things to return to normalcy.

We are back, of course, to the elementary principle stated early in this book: if we assume the best about our people they will do everything they can to live up to those expectations. The astonishing opportunity facing us is that we can call out almost any aspect of another we wish. That even includes calling out the rational, productive self in those who are temporarily giving us a hard time.

"Nothing great or new can be done without enthusiasm. Enthusiasm is the fly-wheel which carries your saw through the knots in the log. A certain excessiveness seems a necessary element in all greatness."
—Dr. Harvey Cushing

CHAPTER THIRTEEN

The Personality of the Motivator

We must now address the topic of charisma. What is it about the personality and character of certain persons that enables them to inspire others? It obviously does not require superior looks, an expensive education, or a privileged birth, for as we look back upon the leaders who have brought out our full potential, we note that few of them had those advantages. To be a successful leader of people requires only two things: (1) an astute knowledge of what makes people tick; and (2) a spirit that spreads excitement and energy to other people.

The latter quality can be acquired just as much as the former, but unfortunately it can also be lost very readily. In other words, this is an ingredient of the inner person which requires regular maintenance. So the final rule for bringing out the best in people is this:

Take Steps to Keep Your Own Motivation High

Certain persons lead the pack early, then fail to fulfill their promise. On the other hand, certain persons who were loners in their earlier years can become very strong and very successful leaders. This is doubtless due in part to the spirit they had cultivated in those silent years.

Independence as an Ingredient of Charisma

In fact, one could make a case for the proposition that all great leaders are loners. Contrary to what some think, the outstanding motivators are not necessarily the gregarious, backslapping types at all. Rather, they often spend a great deal of time alone, thinking and planning.

In order to lead, it is simply imperative to have independence. Psychologist Nathaniel Branden has said:

> Innovators and creators are persons who can to a higher degree than average accept the condition of aloneness. They are more willing to follow their own vision even when it takes them far from the mainland of the human community. Unexplored spaces do not frighten them— or as much as they frighten those around them. This is one of the secrets of their power. That which we call "genius" has a great deal to do with courage and daring, a great deal to do with *nerve*.

So it is a mistake to attempt to be "one of the boys" in order to lead. If we examine the personalities of people like Florence Nightingale, Churchill, Napoleon, de Gaulle, Martin Luther, and Mother Teresa, we cannot escape the conclusion that these people have been quite eccentric. And to some extent, this very eccentricity helps get them recognized as leaders.

The cultivation of charisma seems to require a certain amount of solitude. Tom J. Fatjo Jr. parlayed an investment of $500 into a fortune while still in his 30s and then went on to found the Houstonian, a center for personal renewal. He finds it necessary to spend a day each week running and being totally alone, usually at his beach house, so that he can assure himself he has simplified his life and moved forward toward his goals. It was Carl Sandburg's speculation about Lincoln that his greatness came in part from the years spent in the woods with that solitary companion, the ax.

Jesus' life was checkered with solitude. The New Testament says with succinct eloquence that before a busy day of healing and teaching, "in the morning, a great while before day, he rose and went out to a lonely place, and there he prayed."

Later that same morning, when Peter found Jesus praying, he greeted him with an interesting remark: "Master, everyone is searching for you." It is an old paradox: independent people who regularly separate themselves from the crowds will often be the ones whom the crowd most wants to follow.

The Motivator as Dreamer

Some commentators think that the day of the strong leader is past and that the model of Japanese management, where people are homogenized and the individuality of the leader is minimized, will become the standard. There are some valuable lessons to be learned from the Japanese, but in the West, at least, most people are looking for bold leaders who will set goals, make decisions, and then breathe vision into the people around them.

On a warm Friday night in April 1961, John F. Kennedy gathered a handful of his closest advisors in the Cabinet Room to ponder the Soviet space challenge. Only two days before, Uri Gagarin had become the first man to go into orbit. Kennedy was 43 years old then, and he seemed 30. A man of little scientific knowledge, he was listening to technicians describe a 10-year, 40-billion-dollar race with no guarantee that America would get to the moon first. Like a boy, Kennedy put his foot on the edge of the cabinet table, fiddled with a loose rubber sole on his shoe, ran his hands through his hair, and ended the meeting with his jaw set.

Fifteen minutes later he sent the word out, "We're going to the moon." *Time* correspondent Hugh Sidey, looking back on that evening, says:

> This was not a military imperative. There was no overwhelming clamor from the public or Congress for such an effort. Something special happened in the mind of Kennedy. The poet in him glimpsed the future, perhaps, or the Irish combativeness responded to the prospects of a race. What we do know is that John Kennedy decided finally, in those few minutes, to take the nation on a peaceful and creative journey the likes of which this world has never known.

Good motivators are willing to think and act in such bold fashion, to set goals far out front of the group. And since there are so few people who will dare to think big and to risk the humiliation of failure, the person who will dare to do so is almost certain to have a following. Goethe said, "Whatever you dream you can, begin it. Boldness has genius, power and magic in it."

Of course we all know persons who talk big and do nothing more. There is such a thing as the useless idealist who is so busy spinning grand schemes that there is no time to bother with smaller goals on the way. If daydreaming becomes a means of avoiding hard work, then it is a liability. Here is the difference: the successful leader dreams boldly and keeps the larger picture always in mind, but is also willing to work at the intermediate steps required for success. Kennedy, for instance, was anything but an empty talker. He had proven his ability to set a goal and achieve it. At first his objectives were to get elected to the House of Representatives and then to the Senate. This was a man who had used his legs as well as his mouth, and when such a person speaks of large dreams, people listen.

It is not all that unusual a quality—this ability to think big, to dream large dreams; most of us do it regularly. Especially as children, we spin fantasies of great achievements. Doubtless one of the reasons that Jesus was forever urging that we become like little children is that they have such a penchant for daydreaming. Their mind is a constant picture screen on which they are staring at fabulous successes.

This ability that Jesus admired in children is equally admirable in business tycoons like Walt Disney, who was successful partially because he never stopped thinking like a child. Mike Vance tells about being at Disneyworld soon after its completion when someone said, "Isn't it too bad Walt Disney didn't live to see this?" Vance replied: "He *did* see it—that's why it's here!" Indeed, the best leaders and the most powerful motivators have been those with an almost defiant ability to envision great things occurring in the future, and to see them happening in great detail.

Putting the Dream into Words

There is another ingredient to charisma—an ability to talk about one's dreams. Although most of us are willing to dream, not all of us are willing to share our dreams with other people. We think about challenging our Sunday school class to double its enrollment or suggesting an expansion plan for our company, but then we picture the doomsayers and the dreamspoilers who will object and tell us it can't be done. We think of the possibility of failing in front of other people, so we don't talk about our dreams. And sure enough, if we keep them to ourselves, our plans probably will not come to fruition. Later, in retrospect, we'll be glad we kept quiet.

But no great achievement has ever occurred without some one person taking the risk of propounding an idea at which others might have laughed. Motivators always use words lavishly and intensely as they outline their dreams to prospective supporters. Such diverse leaders as Lyndon Johnson, Winston Churchill, and Lee Iacocca have all possessed something in common: a mesmerizing ability to talk. Some may have had their shy sides, but when the occasion presented itself, each could pour out a profusion of words.

The successful motivator does far more talking than the average person. We have all heard long dissertations on the wisdom of listening and keeping our mouths shut, and indeed there are heads of corporations who are men and women of few words and who lead their organizations successfully. But they are managers, not persuaders and motivators. Their success is from their organizational ability, and that is another topic.

The inspiring talker produces a zeal, said Aldous Huxley, "whose intensity depends not on the rationality of what is said or the goodness of the cause that is being advocated, but solely on the propagandist's skill [in using] words in an exciting way."

Words are a remarkably powerful vehicle. Much of Franklin D. Roosevelt's success was due to his ability to coin a phrase and to use slogans to summarize his dreams, and those slogans became a part of the fabric of our national life. Gandhi and Martin Luther King Jr. both knew that if one speaks long enough, there is an uplifting and elevating, almost intoxicating power in words. Most of us have experienced it hundreds of times—listening to another speak, either before an audience or in one-to-one conversation, until the sound of their words and the sheer weight of their flow eventually persuades us.

You can gain a considerable following if you are willing to relate your message to enough people and not be deterred by the large numbers who will not buy it. Instead, you pick up your idea and present it to the next prospect. Eventually, with enough presentations to enough people, a few people become enthusiastic, they join the parade, one by one, and soon a movement is on its way. Talk may be cheap, but the right use of words can generate in your followers a commodity impossible to buy: hearts on fire.

The Ability to Defy Criticism

Criticism is never easy for anyone, but it is absolutely essential to acquire some thick armor against it if one is to be a motivator of people. The masses are certain to make negative remarks about every worthwhile scheme and the good leader will be braced for such shortsighted thinking.

I am not advocating either arrogance or an unwillingness to listen to the counsel of others. There is a fine line between the courage of one's convictions on the one hand and on the other the grandiosity we see in some who, upon achieving some status, decide that they are now beyond reproach. The Greek tragedians called it *hubris,* and it still wrestles people to the floor. Everyone, no matter how highly placed, needs to be accountable to a few people, and the wise leaders always have some colleagues who will tell them when they are about to make fools of themselves.

No American better illustrates the ideal balance than Abraham Lincoln. He was viciously attacked by the Eastern press and, being a sensitive and wise man, he did not ignore his critics. Yet he knew that he could be debilitated if he tried to please everyone. So he reportedly posted this sign:

> If I were to try to read, much less answer, all the attacks made on me, this shop might as well be closed for any other business. I do the very best I know how—the

very best I can; and I mean to keep doing so until the end.

Most great motivators have been a minority of one in certain situations. Anyone who looks carefully at the biographies of Jesus cannot help being impressed with the loneliness with which he conducted much of his ministry. People did not understand him, they could not stay loyal to him, and eventually they abandoned him. Yet he steadfastly set his face forward and achieved more than anyone who has ever graced the face of this earth.

The Power of Enthusiasm

There is another ingredient to charisma, and it is variously called intensity, obsessiveness, or enthusiasm. But whatever one calls it, we all recognize it as a quality residing in every effective motivator. These leaders attack their projects with an enormous energy. This personality trait is quickly recognized by the crowd and gets attention in a hurry. Emerson said, "Every great and commanding movement in the annals of the world is a triumph of enthusiasm." And the former sales manager for NCR put it this way: "Genius is intensity. The salesman who surges with enthusiasm, though it is excessive, is superior to the one who has no passion. I would prefer to calm down a geyser than start with a mudhole."

It is one of the bromides of the success manuals that enthusiasm is contagious and that you cannot get a group of people fired up unless you are enthusiastic yourself. Such advice can cause some leaders to think they must adopt a continuously cheerful demeanor and appear happy at all times. But such behavior quickly gets recognized as counterfeit, and no one wants to follow a leader who is superficially and artificially happy. I notice that the great leaders get angry at times, and at other times they are depressed and unhappy. On at least one occasion, Jesus could tell his closest aides that he was "overwhelmed with sorrow to the point of death."

So you do not have to be Pollyanna to succeed as a leader. But you *do* have to have a powerful commitment to your goals and your group. You must be able to keep going when others get fainthearted, to throw away the clock until the job is done.

Self-Renewal for the Motivator

What we've been saying in this chapter is that charisma is more a matter of attitude than aptitude. That brings us to the importance of regular self-renewal for the motivating leader. If it is true that the quality of your spirit is the essential thing you bring to your leadership task, then the management of your *own* motivation must take top priority.

How is the motivator motivated? Here are five suggestions:

1. Associate with successful, positive people. In some cases you may need to distance yourself somewhat from pessimistic people who pull you down. At least you must be certain to spend considerable time with individuals who inspire you, people who will stimulate your thinking, restore your vision, and stretch your capacity for dreaming. "If you are determined to be successful," says Patricia Fripp, "it is very

important to associate with success-oriented people.''

2. Monitor carefully the ideas entering your mind, for as the computer people say, ''garbage in, garbage out.'' If you become what you think, and if you feed a constant stream of junk and trivia into your brain, you are unlikely to be the strong persuader you want to be. You may need to turn off the TV, watch less news, and instead read the great books, or mull over the powerful ideas of the Bible. The actress Helen Hayes said, ''We rely upon the poets, the philosophers, and the playwrights to . . . illuminate the thoughts for which we only grope; they give us the strength and balm we cannot find in ourselves. Whenever I feel my courage wavering I rush to them. They give me the wisdom of acceptance, the will and resilience to push on.''

3. Take advantage of the wealth of information now available on inexpensive audio cassettes. The wonderful thing about tapes is that in listening to them we get not only the ideas of great people but it is the next best thing to being with them in person— by listening to their voices we have a chance to make contact with their personalities, with their energy and enthusiasm. So rather than letting the radio's stream of nonsense occupy your driving hours or the time when you are waiting, listen to tapes of inspiring and successful people whose stories will elevate your moods. According to a study made at the University of Southern California, if you live in a metropolitan area and drive 12,000 miles each year, in three years' time you can acquire the equivalent of two years of college lectures.

4. Attend classes and seminars. It is worth a few hundred miles of travel and a few hundred dollars to audit courses taught by bright people where you can associate with other highly motivated persons.

The seminar circuit today is the equivalent of the medieval traveling university, and it is possible to get an excellent education there.

5. Keep a journal in which you write down goals and a record of your spiritual journey. A good journal is quite different from a diary. You are not writing down events that happened outside you during the day—rather you are observing and recording the movements of your soul. If this is done consistently, positive dreams and objectives are certain to arise from the unconscious. Freud was rather pessimistic about the unconscious: he thought that in psychotherapy it needed to be uncovered and the unconscious material needed to be aired, but for him it was like taking the lid off a septic tank—there was all manner of dark and horrendous material there. Carl Jung, on the other hand, was much more an optimist about who we are at our deepest level. He believed that when we uncover the unconscious we may find some aberrations and there may be some blackness, but it is our deepest self that is the source of all great art. It is, Jung thought, the source of all things beautiful and creative, and it is a point at which we meet God. If Jung is right, then one of the surest ways to keep our motivation high is to keep open the corridors between our conscious mind and the unconscious mind.

In the end, the ability to give inspiring leadership is an inner quality of spirit; it requires people who, to use Emerson's noble phrase, "live from a great depth of being." And such spirituality does not come upon us suddenly. It accrues gradually from persistent study and regular cultivation.

*"Love is a fruit in season at all times,
and within the reach of every hand."*
—MOTHER TERESA OF CALCUTTA

CHAPTER FOURTEEN

Why Helping Other People Grow Can Become Life's Greatest Joy

Our offices are on the top floor of a medical building, and when I sit at my window between appointments with patients, I often ponder the healing of persons in general and the personalities of those in the helping professions in particular. Many of the people with whom I work are themselves doctors, teachers, and social workers who feel beleaguered and weighted down by their tasks. There are so many needy people, they say, with so many problems, and for every person they get patched up, there are dozens of others who are falling apart.

When there are storms out on the Pacific, an occasional sea gull, driven inland by the weather, will swing past my window, gracefully riding the currents. My patients, also, have fled from storms. Their idealism has been battered, and now they are not certain that they can genuinely help anyone. As one clergyman said sadly, "When I went into the ministry I thought I was going to save the world and rescue all these people. But that was a long time ago. Now I'm much more pessimistic about anyone making that much difference and my goals are very simple: all I want to do is survive."

According to the current jargon, these persons are suffering from burnout. They have lost their faith in the human race; their former hope of helping people and relieving suffering has been replaced by pessimism, and they are not even sure that they believe in God any longer.

When despair hangs in my office after a few such conversations, my mind often goes for replenishment to wartime Sweden and the story of a Baptist lathe hand whose name was Johan Eriksson. Though Johan and I never met, I feel that I know him well, for his daughter, Dagny Svensson, was our office manager for many years.

In 1939, trainloads of Jewish children were piling into Sweden, and the boys and girls—some of them only three and four years old—would file off the trains with no belongings except for the large tags around their necks, designating their home city, their name, and their age. They were thin and pale, with large, sunken, brown eyes. From their melancholy gaze it was evident that they had already seen and experienced things far beyond their years—atrocities that most people would never have to see in a lifetime.

The Swedish families were taking in children for "the duration of the war," but few were deluded into thinking that it would be a short time. One of the Swedes who opened his door was Johan Eriksson. He had known deprivation himself—at 28 he had been left a widower with four children. By now he was middle-aged and most of the children were gone. But when he learned that a frightened nine year old named Rolf needed a home, he responded as if he were still a young man. And so a little Jewish boy began to adjust to life in a strict Swedish Baptist home. At first, when there was a knock on the door or loud voices outside, the boy with the deep-set eyes would dive into a closet and cover his head, but he was surrounded with warmth and love in the Eriksson house, and he began to gain weight, to lose the faraway gaze, and eventually he began to laugh again.

When an invasion by the Nazis seemed imminent, men at the machine shop said to Johan, "When Hitler comes you will be in trouble with that Jew boy in your house. They'll come and take him away." The normally gentle Swede would reply with clenched jaw, "They'll never take him so long as I'm alive." And curiously, Johan was almost equally defensive of Rolf before his fellow Baptists. When members of the church assumed that he would try to convert the boy, Johan's jaw would clench again. The Swedish government had promised the refugee organization that the children's religion would be kept intact, and although Johan took little Rolf to church with his family, he went to considerable lengths to see that the boy learned the Jewish tradition and that when the proper age came he was prepared for and celebrated his Bar Mitzvah. When the war ended, Johan wanted to return to Rolf's parents a son who had been raised as closely as possible to the way they would have wanted.

But when the war did end, the family was never reunited, of course. Rolf's parents perished somewhere in Europe along with the millions of others who were killed during those apocalyptic years. Letters from his parents had become more and more sporadic, and then one day an envelope arrived without a postmark. Inside was a hastily scribbled note saying that Rolf would not hear from them again, and that he should never forget what this Swedish family had done for him.

And Rolf did not forget. He grew up and went away to Stockholm, where he began to succeed in business. But the trauma and the wrenching of those early years perhaps took a belated toll, for one day Rolf's mind snapped. Relatives told Johan Eriksson that he had done enough, and the authorities wanted permission to keep the young man in a mental institution, for he was thought to be dangerous. But Johan would have none of it. "He belongs here," he said simply. "This is his home." And so Rolf returned to the little city of Åmål and the quiet, solid Swede took him in again. For a year Johan nursed him until his mind returned to stability and peacefulness.

Rolf's life was relatively untroubled after that. He married, reared children, established his own company, and became very wealthy. But he never forgot the man who had given him such unconditional love when he was a boy. Nothing was ever too good for Johan, and as the old man became more infirm, an even stronger bond seemed to glue them together. If Johan was sick or needed him, Rolf thought nothing of taking the train across Sweden to spend what was left of the weekend with the man who had become like a father. And when Johan was on his deathbed, all the children hurried home, but everyone knew who would arrive first—Rolf.

My mind often returns to the story of Johan and Rolf when I feel the doubt and despair of my fellow therapists. The reason is this: if Johan Eriksson had accomplished no other noteworthy thing in his long life, it surely would have been worth living to have been there to shelter one such child. When we get discouraged in our work with people it is important to draw back and remind ourselves that there is no more noble occupation in the world than to assist another human being, to help someone else succeed.

Power—Its Use and Abuse

As we get older, unfortunately, it is easy to discard the idealism of our earlier years, to withdraw more and more into a safe world, and, after learning to wield power for our advantage, to become manipulators of the people around us. A veritable library is available to assist us in making this manipulative use of power. Books such as *Winning through Intimidation, How to Get the Upper Hand,* and *Getting Your Way* have sold millions of copies in these decades of "me-first" philosophy, and it is quite possible to begin to regard persons around us as mere objects to use—robots whose value we can exchange for money, power, or both.

But now comes a thoughtful book by Robert K. Greenleaf, the retired director of management research for American Telephone and Telegraph. Greenleaf's research shows that the ruthless, self-serving manipulator never succeeds in the long run. The title of Greenleaf's book is itself instructive: *Servant Leadership: A Journey into the Nature of Legitimate Power and Greatness.* Greenleaf argues that "to be a lone chief atop a pyramid is abnormal and corrupting. . . . When someone is moved atop a pyramid, that person no longer has colleagues, only subordinates.''

Greenleaf does not waste much time offering an alternate model to the pyramid. Instead, he addresses the attitude of the leader and makes a strong case that the person in places of authority must assume the attitude of servant. The best business people have always known the importance of that concept. When A. W. Clausen headed the Bank of America, he quipped that he devoted 60% of his time to planning, 60% to people, and all other duties had to take what was left. In our age of high-tech advancement it is very easy to forget that our failure or success will be determined largely by our ability to work with and assist other people in functioning at their best. When Zoltan Merszei left Dow Chemical to become president of Occidental Petroleum, he hired a former Dow colleague as personnel director and, in announcing the job placement, made a telling comment about his own priorities: ''Ron goes along with my philosophy that people make business. Technology is a distant second.''

There is simply no substitute for the rewards of helping other people grow, the pleasures of teaching other people to succeed, and the excitement of organizing a group of colleagues who spark one another's enthusiasm. The idea of such contributory leadership is not entirely new, of course. When Jesus gave his disciples instructions about the style of leadership they would be following, he warned against lording it over others in the manner of their current political bosses. Instead, he said, his disciples would be able to attain greatness by being last, by becoming ''slave of all.'' ''For the

Son of man," he explained, "came not to be served, but to serve."

Recently, before I was to make some remarks to a medical conference in Monterey, California, I met Dr. Arthur Tayengco, who was born in the Philippines and raised in an average, middle-class home. It would have been normal that Arthur would have gone on to an average life himself, except that in the elementary school he attended, there was a Redemptorist priest, Father Ian Madigan—an Irishman with a hearty laugh and with light in his eyes—who took an interest in the little boy. "I don't know where I'd be, if Father Madigan hadn't noticed me and talked to me about my possibilities," says Dr. Tayengco. And so two years ago, Dr. Tayengco made an important pilgrimage. By this time the old priest had retired to his homeland, so the now-famous physician and his wife traveled there to call on the bemused and aging man. "I simply needed to tell him how much I owed to him," says Dr. Tayengco. "You just can't overestimate the influence of a teacher like that."

The Potential in Persons

The old Irish priest was a dogged follower of Christ not only in his servant role, but also in his attitude. In talking to the young boy, he displayed another Christly virtue we've been discussing on and off throughout this book: a tough-minded optimism about the possibilities in the human race. One of the distressing aspects of so much current pessimism in the helping professions is its cynical and bleak view of people in general. When one is dealing with the troubled and the needy it is easy to fall into the trap of assuming that people do not want to rise out of their misery, that they all want to be parasites.

Such a suspicious, on-guard posture is simply unnecessary. Someone asked a hotel manager how many of his patrons turned out to be deadbeats. "Oh, a quarter of one percent," he said. If this proportion were as much as 10%, society would be in terrible trouble. Charge accounts, installment buying, even writing and accepting ordinary checks would be impossible. If it were 25%, society would explode. The fact is, we *can* trust most people.

The wonderful thing about the Bible is that it does not take some Pollyanna view that everything is beautiful and that things will always turn out fine. Tragedy, suffering, and inhumanity do indeed exist, and no world view would be accurate if it did not take into account what Melville called the "blackness of things." All that notwithstanding, the Bible takes the view that men and women are God's good creation. Our self-centeredness often distorts that creation, but people have God-given dignity and goodness. "What is man that thou art mindful of him?" muses the psalmist. "Thou hast made him little less than God, and dost crown him with glory and honor."

Someone has said that one can look at the handicapped and ask, "How could God possibly allow blindness and deafness?" Or one can look at Helen Keller and see her great spirit, her great love, her great accomplishment. When she was given an honorary law degree at the University of Glasgow, she said in response, "It is a sign, Sir, that silence and darkness need not block progress of the immortal human spirit." And one is forced to say that there must be a great God in this world to produce such greatness.

The Grandeur of Service

If it is true that people can grow, expand their capacities, jump higher, run harder, and compose greater music, that means that the ultimate leadership is servant leadership, for we will produce followers who will surpass us. Runners will become coaches and train other athletes who will break their records. Executives will hire subordinates and motivate them so well that they may become their superiors.

It is not easy to adjust to such a view of the development of leaders, and when some people get to the top they pull up the ladder with them. They cannot tolerate the ambition of the young and see every subordinate as a potential rival. Such executives hang on by their fingernails in organizations until the last possible moment and give their attention to fighting off rivals rather than nurturing successors. It is a foolish way to lead, inasmuch as we are always within one generation of extinction.

In my practice I often see parents who compete with their children and fight them when they try to assert their independence. But when a son tries to show his father that he is stronger, it is not only healthy competition—it is also a desire to please his father and repay him for the years of shepherding and teaching. Growing up on a Texas farm, I recall with affection the years when I began to match my father's strength in lifting bags of seed and how he was not at all defeated when I began to carry objects too heavy for him. Rather than resisting the competition, he was obviously proud of me, and with a wide smile he would tell mom at the dinner table how strong her son was becoming. I recall those events with such affection because it is an example of the very best leadership— leadership that believes the best about the people below you, reaches down and pulls them up beside you, and then seeks to push them up even higher.

It is interesting to see how profound is this inter- connection of the generations by observing it in one's own progeny. One day last summer my daughter called from Children's Hospital in Los Angeles. She and her 21-month-old son Christopher had been at the emer- gency room for tests all afternoon. She sobbed, "They're admitting him, and they think it's menin- gitis."

We raced to the hospital, then went from one floor to another, searching for them. When we finally spied her at the far end of a long corridor, the scene etched a picture in my brain that will be vivid for as long as I live. Sharon was carrying Christopher, unconscious, in her arms, his legs and arms dangling like limp wil- low limbs after a storm. His fingers and toes were still blue. His grandmother walked on one side, holding the IV bottle high so he could continue to get the vital flow of medication as they walked, and on the other side was a nurse, carrying his chart. When I saw that little group hurrying toward us, primal emotions of love, loyalty, fear, intimacy, and the protective instinct all mingled in a moment. But most profound was the awareness that after these years when we were the parents and in charge, my daughter was now the par- ent. She was the one making decisions and taking care of her young, and I was there primarily to watch.

As we lived through those weeks until Christopher recovered, and as I watched my daughter's devotion to him in the hospital room 24 hours a day, I was in awe of the potent maternal instinct in her that could be gentle and succoring to her baby when necessary and also ferocious and protecting like a mother bear when necessary. Here was Sharon—who seemed to have been a tiny, frizzy-haired little toddler herself so recently and whose adult life at times had been unfocused and meandering—now powerfully concentrated with an overwhelming and fierce determination that her son was going to live, that he was going to get the best medical care possible, and that he would never awake once during those weeks and be frightened because his mother had gone home. Here was my little girl so determined that her son would live that she almost literally kept him from dying during those early touch-and-go days.

As I watched those scenes, it furnished me with an instructive metaphor for a fundamental fact about leadership: we lead best when we seek the welfare of those we lead, when we seek to serve rather than being served. The devotion of a parent to a child—the combination of protecting them and pushing them out of the nest—is the epitome of leadership, and it is the best example of motivating without manipulating.

In fact, when the early biblical writers sought for an analogy with which to describe the relationship between God and creation, it was this very connection that was chosen. God is our heavenly Father, a loving, prodding, protecting, and coaching parent.

It is not always easy for the concerned parent, the idealistic teacher, the high-spirited executive to be tolerant of those we lead. The people who live in our houses and inhabit our offices are sometimes less ambitious than we are, sometimes less sure of themselves, sometimes less gifted. They are, like us, a mixture of the bad and the good. But if we can reach in and draw out the best from them—if we can, like Vince Lombardi, challenge them to give an extra 10%—they will try harder for us than for anyone in the world, and they will accomplish some surprising things. That extra 10% just may be the difference that wins the game.

Notes

pp. 19-20   Sandra Day O'Connor material, *People Weekly*, October 12, 1981, p. 51.

pp. 30-31   C. Knight Aldrich, "Thief," *Psychology Today*, March 1971, pp. 67-69.

pp. 32-33   Robert Rosenthal and Lenore Jacobson, *Pygmalion in the Classroom* (New York: Holt, Rinehart and Winston, 1968). For a superb discussion of this topic, see Robert Coles's review in *The New Yorker*, April 19, 1969, pp. 169-177.

p. 38   William James, "The Energies of Men," *Memories and Studies* (New York: Longmans, Green, and Co., 1917), pp. 237-238.

pp. 38-39   Helen Erskine, "The Most Unforgettable Character I've Met," *The Reader's Digest*, November 1953, p. 43.

pp. 43-44   Frank Bettger, *How I Raised Myself from Failure to Success in Selling* (Englewood Cliffs, N.J.: Prentice-Hall, 1947), p. 50. © 1947 by Prentice-Hall, Inc. Renewed 1977 by Frank Bettger. Reprinted by permission of the publisher.

p. 53   Alan Alda quotation in Elizabeth Kaye, "Arlene and Alan Alda: A Love Story," *McCalls*, January 1976, p. 16.

p. 56   Thomas J. Peters and Robert H. Waterman Jr., *In Search of Excellence* (New York: Harper & Row, 1982), p. 77.

p. 58   Bill Honig quote in William Body, "Answer Man," *California Magazine*, September 1973, p. 78.

pp. 59-61   Mario M. Cuomo, *Diaries of Mario M. Cuomo: The Campaign for Governor* (New York: Random House, 1984), pp. 333-334. Copyright © 1984 by Mario M. Cuomo. Reprinted by permission of Random House Inc.

pp. 61-62   Kenneth Blanchard and Spencer Johnson, *The One-Minute Manager* (New York: William Morrow, 1982.)

p. 62   Dan Rather quote in *The Camera Never Blinks* (New York: William Morrow, 1973), p. 25.

pp. 69-70   Albert L. Rowse, *The Churchills* (New York: Harper & Row, 1958), p. 381. I am also indebted to Dr. Rowse for other details about Dunkirk.

p. 72   Charles Knight quotation in *Time*, February 25, 1980, p. 82.

p. 79   Kennedy and Roosevelt anecdotes in Ralph G. Martin, *A Hero for Our Time* (New York: Macmillan, 1983), p. 23.

pp. 83-84   Leon Festinger, *A Theory of Cognitive Dissonance* (Evanston: Row, Peterson, 1975).

pp. 84-85   Jonathan L. Freedman and Scott C. Fraser, "Compliance without Pressure: The Foot-in-the-Door Technique," *Journal of Personality and Social Psychology* 4 (1966): 195-202.

p. 87   James Dobson, *Hide or Seek* (Old Tappan, N.J.: Fleming H. Revell Co., 1974), p. 11. This is a superb, easy-to-read book on strategies for improving your child's self-esteem.

p. 99   Terrence E. Deal and Allan A. Kennedy, *Corporate Cultures* (Reading, Mass.: Addison-Wesley, 1982), p. 37.

p. 106   Peters and Waterman, *In Search of Excellence*, p. 58.

p. 108   Ibid., pp. 70-71

p. 109   Karen Pryor, *Don't Shoot the Dog* (New York: Simon and Schuster, 1984), p. 46. Copyright © 1984 by Karen Pryor. Reprinted by permission of Simon and Schuster, Inc. and the Julian Bach Literary Agency, Inc.

pp. 114-115   Excerpts from "Where Success Comes From" by Arthur Gordon, copyright © 1960 by Arthur Gordon. Used by permission of the author. All rights reserved.

pp. 118-119   Roland G. Tharp and Ronald Gallimore, "What a Coach Can Teach a Teacher," *Psychology Today*, January 1976, pp. 75-78.

p. 121   Victor Cline, *How to Make Your Child a Winner* (New York: Walker and Co., 1980), p. 120.

p. 121   The story of Claire is from Wesley Baker, *Parents Are Teachers* (Champaign, Ill.: Research Press, 1971), pp. 129-130.

NOTES

p. 122   Karen Pryor, *Don't Shoot the Dog*, pp. 143,144.

p. 122   James Q. Wilson, "Raising Kids," *The Atlantic Monthly*, October 1983, p. 53.

pp. 126-127   Charles Schwab quotation in Dale Carnegie, *How to Win Friends and Influence People* (New York: Pocket Books, 1975), pp. 182-183. Copyright © 1936 by Dale Carnegie, renewed © 1969 by Donna Dale Carnegie and Dorothy Carnegie. Reprinted by permission of Simon and Schuster, Inc.

pp. 129-130   The quotations from Arno Penzias are from the book by Jeremy Bernstein, *Three Degrees above Zero*. Copyright © 1984 Jeremy Bernstein. Originally appeared in the August 20, 1984 issue of *The New Yorker*. Reprinted with the permission of *The New Yorker* and Charles Scribner's Sons.

pp. 132-133   The Lee Iacocca excerpt is quoted by permission.

pp. 142-143   Morgan W. McCall Jr. and Michael M. Lombardo, "What Makes a Top Executive?" *Psychology Today*, February 1983, p. 28.

pp. 146-147   Bank of America information is from *Harvard Business Review*, January-February 1980, pp. 109-110.

p. 154   Robert R. Updegraff quotation is from his book *Yours to Venture* (New York: McGraw-Hill, 1937), p. 72.

p. 162   Nathaniel Branden, *The Psychology of Romantic Love* (Los Angeles: J. P. Tarcher, 1980), p. 61. Copyright © 1980 by Nathaniel Branden, Ph.D. Reprinted by permission of Bantam Books Inc.

p. 164   Hugh Sidey, column in *Time*, Nov. 17, 1980. Copyright 1980 Time Inc. All rights reserved. Reprinted by permission from Time.

pp. 168-169   Lincoln quotation in John Barlett, *Familiar Quotations*, 13th ed. (Boston: Little, Brown, 1955), p. 542.

pp. 177-178   Robert K. Greenleaf, *Servant Leadership: A Journey into the Nature of Legitimate Power and Greatness* (New York: Paulist Press, 1977, p. 63.

p. 178   Mark 10:44-45 RSV.

p. 180   Psalm 8:4-5 RSV.

Index of Names

Dr. Alan Loy McGinnis

"At last! An easy to understand
and easy to apply *book on leadership."*

—Carolyn Savage, senior national sales director
Mary Kay Cosmetics

*"Anyone but a hermit would benefit from reading
this book. It is 'must reading' for executives."*

—James R. Schultz, vice president
Spencer Stuart & Associates, San Francisco

"Clear insight, time after time."
—Kenneth R. Larson, regional director
Phoenix Mutual Life Insurance Company